To Your Good Health!

Dr Thomas Stuttaford was born in 1931 in rural Norfolk where his father and grandfather had been general practitioners. He joined the family practice in 1959 after completing his national service with the Tenth Royal Hussars and medical training at Oxford and in London.

In 1970 Dr Stuttaford left the Norfolk practice and became the Conservative MP for Norwich South. During this time he continued to work as a doctor in London. In 1974 Dr Stuttaford resumed full-time medical practice, but found the time to contest the Isle of Ely both in that year and in 1979.

Dr Stuttaford has been interested in alcohol, as a doctor and consumer, since his army and university days. His conviction that a moderate consumption of alcohol is beneficial has not been blunted by his experience of caring for patients who were either drug or alcohol dependent.

Since leaving politics Dr Stuttaford has divided his time between occupational health and genito-urinary medicine – at the Royal London Hospital, Moorfields Eye Hospital and the former Queen Mary's Hospital for the East End – and medical journalism. Dr Stuttaford is at present *The Times'* doctor; he has been writing for the paper for fifteen years. He is also a regular contributor to *The Oldie* magazine, and has in the past been the medical correspondent to *Options* and *Elle* magazines.

Amongst Dr Stuttaford's other enthusiasms are the restoration of old buildings and the preservation of the countryside. He has been instrumental in restoring six listed Norfolk houses, and is at present living in a 300-year-old house in Elm Hill, the most ancient of Norwich's streets. He is married to Pamela Ropner, also a writer, and has three sons.

To Your Good Health!

The Wise Drinker's Guide

Dr Thomas Stuttaford

faber and faber

LONDON · BOSTON

First published in 1997
by Faber and Faber Limited
3 Queen Square London WC1N 3AU

Typeset by Faber and Faber Ltd
Printed in England by Clays Ltd, St Ives plc

A CIP record for this book
is available from the British Library

ISBN 0–571–19095–2

2 4 6 8 10 9 7 5 3 1

To all moderate drinkers

Contents

Acknowledgements

The author would like to thank family, friends, colleagues and patients who have contributed knowingly or unknowingly to this book:

My wife, who has nobly supported me and tolerated my preoccupation with the book with good humour. Special thanks to my son Thomas, who has gleaned interesting facts from obscure libraries in Paris, but to all three of my sons for their advice on the book – and for accepting my assurance from an early age that two to four glasses of red wine was good for them long before it was, once again, a respectable medical opinion.

Julian Jeffs, eminent lawyer, bon viveur and expert on wine, for his patience, understanding and unflagging enthusiasm for the book, regardless of the length of its gestation. Thanks, too, to Belinda Matthews of Faber and Faber, whose experience, reassuring presence and tolerance made writing the book a pleasure.

My medical colleagues, who during my fifteen years with *The Times* have never failed to give generously of their time while they explain some interesting, but complex, clinical fact. Their advice and freely offered opinions have helped to make this book possible.

Dr William Frankland, who kindly briefed me on alcohol and allergy, and whose knowledge on this and allied subjects has helped me not only in my writing but also in the treatment of my patients.

The CBA, which has proved an invaluable source of the information and statistics which were needed to substantiate some of my more controversial statements.

The Medical Council on Alcoholism and the Health Education

To Your Good Health!

Authority for their help and advice, and for the use of their charts and tables.

Very special thanks are due to Annabel Anderson. Her help with collating the research material, and her enthusiasm for the project, have been fundamental to its completion.

Introduction

Doctors' views on alcohol hardened in the thirty years between 1960 and 1990, and reached a point where medical orthodoxy favoured near-abstinence. It was only during those years that alcohol, even in moderate amounts, became to be almost universally condemned by the medical hierarchy. The medical profession sees more of the ill-effects of excessive drinking than anyone else, which understandably stiffens their view. Many felt that the only way to prevent alcoholism was to discourage *everybody* from drinking. Research has, however, finally influenced medical opinion to the point where most doctors are now aware that, under ordinary circumstances, alcohol taken in moderation is life-prolonging as well as life-enhancing.

Even now, despite alcohol's proven value when taken in moderation, it is rarely recommended to a patient. This condemnation has had its disadvantages, and has persuaded many patients to lie about their true drinking habits when talking to their doctors. It is an interesting paradox that, whereas the British consumption of alcohol as a whole has nearly doubled per person in the last thirty years, the amount of drinking admitted by the patient to a doctor in the surgery has fallen steadily.

The opinion which formerly prevailed amongst the medical profession is exemplified by one distinguished professor of medicine at a London teaching hospital. The professor was as kindly as he was knowledgeable, and as a result many of the patients presented him with a bottle when they left the ward. When accepting the present, the doctor was careful to thank the patient profusely for the kind thought, and would then lead him to the nearest basin where, to the horror of the junior staff, the bottle would be emptied down the drain. As the contents ebbed away,

1

the professor would say, 'This is the best place for all drink.'

It is often observed, however, that in so far as drinking is concerned, many doctors have over the last few years found it difficult to follow the advice they have given their patients. The fame of hospital parties does not rest on the quality of their orange juice, and many of the medical magazines carry alluring advertisements for wine prominently displayed amongst those publicizing the latest medicines.

Fashions in medicine are cyclical, and the advice given by my father and grandfather is once again acceptable. It gives me pleasure to know that my advocacy of alcohol in moderation echoes that of my grandfather, who started to practise in the Victorian era. Having been at Cambridge in the 1880s, he had his own practice in Norfolk ten years later. My father, too, was an undergraduate at Cambridge at the end of the nineteenth century, and he continued to work in medicine, although latterly rather inter-

"YOU WANTED TO SEE ME, DOCTOR"

mittently, until the early 1950s. At no time would he have condemned drinking in moderation; in fact, he recommended it, in
spite of his disapproval of drunkenness. Once we were in our
teens we were always given beer with our lunch, and I still
remember the pride I felt when he first asked me to join him for
his regular nightcap of whisky.

This book aims to give a twentieth-century explanation for my
grandfather's nineteenth-century observation that two or three
drinks daily are every bit as efficient at keeping the doctor away
as the proverbial apple. It will also recount how Victorian doctors were fully aware of the hazards of too much alcohol, and
were as keen to warn their patients of the dangers as their successors are today. The horrible effects of alcohol that can ravage
the body and mind of the excessive drinker are described, but it
is comforting to know that what was considered excessive by
opinion-forming doctors five years ago is generally now thought
to be too mean, and their strictures against drinking too severe.

The oft-observed advantages to the cardiovascular system, as
well as the occasional disadvantages, are well documented: a
large number of scientific papers support the concept that alcohol in moderate quantities will provide some protection to most
people's hearts and arteries.

Less often described are the other benefits that accrue to people who drink in moderation. Few people realize that modest
drinkers are less likely to develop non-insulin dependent diabetes; that although heavy drinking increases the likelihood of
developing some cancers, occasional drinking reduces the incidence of others; and that overall mortality is reduced by moderate drinking. This last benefit still holds true even if the
advantages of such drinking to the cardiovascular system are
excluded from the formula.

The benefits to the heart and arteries are most obvious in regular drinkers of red wine, but all alcohol, if not taken to excess, has
a good effect on health. The efficacy of wines varies according to
the type of grape, the soil, the weather and the way in which the
wine is made.

3

Until the second half of this century alcohol, when drunk in small quantities, was thought to be beneficial and the doctor considered it part of his duty not only to discuss the amount drunk, but also the type. The diaries written by the British Ambassador to France in 1909, when King Edward VII was taken dangerously ill in Biarritz, exemplify the Edwardian approach to the use of alcohol in medicine. Sir James Reid, the royal physician and a dour Scot, prescribed 'some nice, light hock' to help the King as he fought for breath. The King's favourite drinks were rather stronger – champagne and brandy – but fortunately the doctor's instructions were interpreted by the royal household to include Rudersheimer, a German wine, but not a very light one. The King recovered.

King George III was another monarch whose disease may have been influenced by alcohol. Everyone who has seen the film *The Madness of King George* will remember that he had acute intermittent porphyria, causing severe abdominal pain, nausea,

" TOO MUCH CHAMPAGNE MR. JONES "

vomiting, constipation, abdominal distension and a host of psychiatric symptoms. It is always a puzzle as to what precipitates an attack, but it is known that alcohol is one substance which may do so. Alan Bennett, the author, does not indicate whether the King's relapses and remissions were in any way related to his alcoholic intake.

Wine drinking still receives royal support. The King of Thailand credits his recovery from a recent illness to the prescription of two glasses of red wine a day. The King now exhorts his subjects to follow his example, and their immediate obedience to his wishes is threatening to create a drought of red wine. It is reported that Thais are buying stakes in the Australian wine fields so that this demand may be met and fortunes made. The Thais are also buying through British shippers.

The UK Department of Health has just increased its recommended safe limits for drinking. For the past few years it had supported the recommendation of the Royal Colleges which govern British medicine that women should not have more than fourteen units in a week and men twenty one units. The limits have now been modified by the Department to twenty-one and twenty-eight units in a week, and not more than four in any one day, with the advice so phrased as to make people aware that it is considered unwise to take all of one's weekly ration in one or two binges.

There is mounting evidence worldwide that the recommendations for both men and women are still more restrictive than they need be. The Department of Health is understandably cautious; it would not want to be accused of encouraging alcoholism, and so has had to draft its advice in such a way that it applies to a wide spectrum of people. Its target audience has to include the short, overweight and tubby men and women who metabolize alcohol badly as well as the giants and the amazons whose natural capacity is much greater. The government's advice must cater for the masses, and so, understandably, does not make allowance for the variations in alcohol tolerance which occur in individuals.

When discussing alcohol intake, the government uses the term 'units'. Although this description is now becoming standard, it is

" WELL HE HAS CUT DOWN TO ONE BOTTLE A DAY, DOCTOR."

still open to misunderstanding. In medical terms, a unit of alcohol is half a pint of beer or cider, a glass of wine or a tot (a standard pub measure) of spirits. The difficulty arises because wine is of very variable strength and glasses are of different sizes. When units of wine are being discussed in this book, a 'glass' will be of the type in which wine would be served in a public house. It is not the cut-glass goblet which graces the dinner table of a generous hostess.

The strength of standard table wines varies from 9 to 13 per cent. Many Spanish wines, for example, are 13 per cent, and some are even stronger. When the waiter brings the bottle to the table for you to check the wine and the vintage, it is also as well to glance at the bottom of the label to check the strength of the alcohol in the wine. Only when armed with this knowledge can you assess the kick of any particular wine, anticipate the effect each glass may have on your ability to drive home, and be forewarned of the influence it could have on behaviour during the evening.

I was once dining with a beloved elderly aunt whose favourite wines were light and German, whereas our host preferred burgundy. A German hock may contain 9 per cent of alcohol by volume, whereas a burgundy is at least 12 per cent; occasionally some of the cheaper French table wines are only 10.9 per cent. By the time we reached the cheese, my elderly relative had had her customary number of glasses and appeared perfectly sober, but

The Relative Strengths of Alcoholic Drinks
From the Health Education Council, London.

The order of strength, in terms of the concentration of absolute alcohol (ethyl alcohol), in spirits, fortified wines, table wines and beer.

40%	**20%**	**10%**	**5%**
Brandy, Gin, Whisky	Fortified wine (Sherry, Port etc)	Table wine	Beer/Cider

Some stronger beers, such as special lagers, contain 8% alcohol. Comparing normal measures of drinks, the following are all approximately equivalent in strength, i.e. in the amount of absolute alcohol they contain. They are all equivalent to 1 unit of alcohol (10ml or 8gm of alcohol approx.)

 = = = =

½ pint of beer	1 glass of table wine	1 glass of sherry	1 single whisky	1 unit of alcohol

she had of course drunk far more alcohol than she was used to. Like many women of her generation, she was too inhibited and controlled to allow her intoxication to show, but as she leant across for the Cheddar she tapped me on the knee and whispered in my ear, 'Tom, I am afraid I can no longer stand. Can you please make the necessary arrangements?'

Just as there is room for error in estimating the amount of alcohol taken when drinking wine, so it is that when drinking beer and spirits other snares are uncovered when totting up the evening's score.

" WOULD YOU LIKE A SMALL UNIT
OR A LARGE UNIT ? "

Beer, like wine, varies greatly in strength. Tennents Super Lager is 9 per cent alcohol by volume, as is Carlsberg Special Brew; both are as strong as a hock, but are drunk in rather different ways and circumstances to wine. At 10.9 per cent, Gold Label Strong Ale is as powerful as many wines. The premium strength beers vary between 4 and 6 per cent alcohol; Guinness, for instance, is 4.1 per cent, Guinness Extra is 4.3 per cent, Murphys 4 per cent,

Units of alcohol per beverage measure

Beer, lager and cider

Approx strengths: % of alcohol by volume	Small can ½ pint (284ml)	Standard can 440 ml	Large can 1 pint (568ml)	Flagon 1 ltr
Low: <1.2% Mild: 2.5%		Whitbread mild *1 unit*	Tennent's LA *1 unit*	
Ordinary: 3.5%	Foster's Lager *1 unit*	Whitbread Pale *1.5 units*	Carlsberg Lager *2 units*	
Export/Strong: 5.0%	Foster's Lager (375 ml) *2 units*	Newquay Premium *2.5 units*	Tennent's Extra (500 ml) *2.5 units*	
		Strongbow cider *2.5 units*	Scrumpy Jack Cider *3 units*	Strongbow cider *5.5 units*
Special/ Super: 9%	Diamond White cider *2 units*	Carlsberg Special Brew *4 units*	Tennent's Super *4.5 units*	Merrydown cider *8 units*

Wines and spirits

	Standard measure	Home measure	Bottle	Litre
Burgundy/ Claret: 12.5%	125 ml *1.5 units*	*2 units*	75 cl *9 units*	1 Litre *12 units*
Sherry/ Port: 18%	60 ml *1 unit*	*2 units*	*13.5 units*	*18 units*
Whisky: 40%	25 ml *1 unit*	*2 units*	70 cl *28 units*	*40 units*

1 unit = 10 ml alcohol-by-volume = 8 g alcohol.

Stones Best Bitter 4.1 per cent, Ruddles County 5 per cent and the premium lagers between 4 per cent and 5 per cent. Standard strength beers and lagers are 3 per cent to 4 per cent alcohol by volume, and low alcohol beers and lagers are 0.9 per cent to 1.2 per cent. A glass of beer may therefore vary in strength from 0.9 per cent to 11 per cent. Cider strength ranges from 1.4 per cent to 8.5 per cent; stronger ones are available, but Customs and Excise regards these as being wine rather than cider.

Be warned about spirits: the measure varies between Scotland, England and Wales; the European Union has a standard measure; in clubs the tot is bigger than it is in pubs and many hotels and restaurants routinely serve doubles. There is a story told in the Reform Club that the larger tot was introduced to St James's clubs by Gladstone. Having travelled down from Scotland, where the pub measure was bigger than in England, and feeling weary, he was shocked by how mean his drink was compared to those served north of the Border. Gladstone complained to the Reform Club committee and thereafter a 'club measure' was introduced, which approximated to that which a politician would be accustomed to in Scotland. When describing a unit of spirits, however, the government is not concerned with Gladstone's needs and uses the standard public house measure.

The average glass of table wine, half-pint of beer or measure of spirits increases the blood alcohol level by 15 mg per 100 ml. Blood alcohol is measured in milligrams per 100 millilitres. Just over three units is usually considered by doctors to be the amount which loosens the inhibitions to the point where judgement may be impaired in someone who is unused to drinking. This amount will give a blood alcohol level of 50 mg per 100 ml. There have been calls to reduce the legal limit for driving to 50 mg (rather than the current 80 mg), because at this level the accident rate increases threefold for drivers who are not used to drinking.

The argument against reduction is that at this level of alcohol there is no discernible effect on the driving, and a negligible influence on the accident figures, of those who are regular, modest drinkers. The breathalyser measures the amount of alcohol in the breath rather than the blood; the number of drinks needed to push the blood alcohol to 80 mg per 100 ml would raise the reading on the breathalyser to 35 mg per 100 ml. The level is lower because by the time the alcohol is excreted in the breath some of it has been metabolized by the liver.

Individuals need to find out for themselves with what alcohol consumption they feel comfortable and how much they can take before their behaviour is affected. Age, gender and size all play a part in a person's capacity to handle alcohol. It is probable that just as in some families a suspect digestive system is inherited, so in others an efficient – or possibly an inefficient – enzyme system for metabolizing alcohol may be passed down through the generations. Just as regular training not only makes the muscles of athletes bigger, but improves their physiological performance, so regular drinking improves the speed and efficiency with which the body deals with alcohol. Some professions and jobs carry with them an increased risk of heavy drinking. The league table is, however, changing.

Nowhere has the change in drinking patterns been more marked than in the City of London. The change was precipitated by the influx of foreign financial houses. The newcomers arrived from all four corners of the world, but the American influence, with its emphasis on long hours and optimum performance, prevailed, leading to dry offices and sandwich luncheons eaten hastily over the desk. It might have been very different if French banking culture had predominated, where in some financial houses the long lunch is still *de rigueur*. The danger which now faces the City man whose thirst is satisfied by water throughout the week is that he may have a heavy drinking session each Friday. Binge drinking and the problems it can cause are dealt with later in the book.

The American pattern of drinking has changed in the last generation too. Although the US businessman may no longer have dry martinis for his lunch, the nation's wine consumption has doubled and they are drinking rather less spirits. The French, on the other hand, now drink less wine; the Mediterranean fondness for wine is thought to account, in part, for the region's low incidence of coronary arterial disease.

City financiers and industrial leaders are not the only people who became notorious for enjoying generous hospitality in the past. Doctors also had a reputation for being heavy drinkers, even if they cannot drink while on duty. Their drinking habits are acquired in their student days, and ever after their opinions

"HEY MAYBE YOU'RE RIGHT — THIS COMPANY DOES NEED AN ALCOHOL POLICY"

on alcohol, when favourable, are apt to be regarded with a degree of suspicion. An illustration of this occurred when, during my brief spell in the House of Commons, a fellow member who was also a doctor rose in defence of a minister accused of being drunk while conducting important business in the House. Unfortunately, the medical MP started his speech with the words, 'As a doctor . . .' The House never did hear the supposed clinical explanation for the minister's unusual behaviour and unsteady gait. The thought of a doctor – particularly this member, who had a reputation for enjoying good living – giving a reasonable judgement on drinking was so improbable that all the members present, on both sides of the House, dissolved into laughter and the incident was forgotten.

The tradition in the House of Commons is that, in the eyes of their colleagues, members are never drunk. However intoxicated an MP might appear to the rest of the world, his or her fellow members do not accuse them of being inebriated. There are many euphemisms – all of which have been employed in the House – to describe the condition of someone who has taken alcohol in greater quantities and more quickly than the liver can metabolize it. The immediate effect of alcohol on the central nervous system is to quicken the thought processes and lighten the mood, but if drinking continues, its influence on behaviour is such that even the regular drinker will in time, like the minister, become 'tired and emotional', the euphemism employed by *Private Eye*. The effect of alcohol on the central nervous system is also discussed later.

Although binge drinking heavy enough to make someone obviously drunk has its own dangers, so too does an immoderate regular consumption. Most heavy drinkers, however, will never suffer from cirrhosis of the liver, for it is only a very small minority who, for some unexplained biochemical reasons, have livers which react in this way to an excessive alcohol intake.

The tragedy is that many of those who do develop cirrhosis probably do so without ever drinking in a way that promotes anti-social behaviour. They are unaware that their excessive consumption is causing damage until the disease is well developed. Cirrhosis in its early stages is unfortunately often without detectable, specific symptoms; the condition may only be noticed by chance at a routine medical. Other sufferers may only have been aware that they were feeling unusually tired and weary. The heavy drinker has probably rarely, if ever, been unpleasantly drunk, but may well have taken for twenty years or more rather too much too often of his favourite tipple, and this regular soaking has slowly destroyed his liver. John le Mesurier, beloved by millions as Sgt Wilson of *Dad's Army*, died suddenly from a ruptured oesophageal varix, a varicose vein at the bottom of the gullet, which is a complication of long-standing cirrhosis. All those wonderful performances he gave must have been filmed even as his liver was slowly being destroyed. Looking back at the repeats recently, I could see that he was looking increasingly unwell as the series progressed; presumably he was unaware of it.

When I was a houseman on a medical unit we admitted a patient dying of acute hepatitis. The senior registrar on the team caught the disease from her and was off work for many months. He gave up hospital practice and became medical adviser to a large firm. For the rest of his life our paths constantly crossed and we often had lunch together, at which we always enjoyed a bottle of wine. He never complained of any subsequent illness, but he, like John le Mesurier, collapsed and died suddenly from a ruptured oesophageal vein. The post mortem showed advanced cirrhosis; another victim of the silent killer, but in the doctor's case the cirrhosis was more likely to have been a result of his attack of hepatitis than heavy drinking.

Most heavy drinkers, if regularly drunk, can expect not only immediate problems from the physical hazards of accidents when intoxicated, but also lasting damage to their health. During my parliamentary days there was an ex-minister, charming and hard-working, who was keen not to use his age and his health, which had been undermined by love of claret, as an excuse to miss votes held in the early hours of the morning. Unfortunately, he was never quite at his best in the small hours, and night after night I was called in to check his condition. Finally we managed to persuade him to be less conscientious in his duties, but only after he had fallen down some steps on his way to vote and glass from his broken spectacles had lacerated both eyelids and cheeks.

Approximately 90 per cent of men and 80 per cent of women in this country enjoy drinking alcohol from time to time. Only a tiny fraction drink to excess; few would ever fall down any steps (especially the hallowed ones in the Palace of Westminster) and a couple of pints two or three nights a week will not turn most people into drunken hooligans. Opponents of drinking are selective in their reporting: they seize upon the disasters which overtake the minority who drink too much and draw conclusions from their behaviour and health which are then applied to the population as a whole. This way of generating statistics is unsound, and their misleading of the public is unjustifiable. The medical advantages of alcohol have been hidden from the general public for thirty years, and the reason usually advanced for this obfuscation is the patronising one that alcohol, delightful as it is to take and good as it is for the heart, cannot be entrusted to the masses lest they drink themselves to death.

The history of teetotalism is interesting. Nowadays we are usually taught that the opposition to drinking had its origins in campaigns to preserve the health of the nation. In fact, in Britain and America, as in ancient Rome, anxiety about alcohol centred not so much on the physical as on the moral and political health of the people. In Rome, Bacchanalian celebrations were seen as established religious festivities and any louche behaviour which accompanied them was accepted. So great is the feeling of exhilaration reached at a crucial point during drinking that the Ancients thought that it was a divine sensation; as the Romans expressed it, they thought at that moment their gods had entered into their soul. Bacchanalian celebrations became so popular that the Consuls feared they would become hotbeds of political intrigue and revolution. Later, even the Methodists accepted that drinking alcohol added to the quality of life – until it began to be supplied from places which attracted a clientele of women of easy virtue.

What was true of the Methodist movement this side of the Atlantic also applied during an earlier age in the United States, where the Puritans initially extolled the health-giving virtues of alcohol. The opposition to alcohol in Muslim countries, usually thought to have been entirely based on its disinhibitory effect, was also on health grounds. Alec Waugh's book *In Praise of Wine* explores the Muslim approach to alcohol; although he claims that the devout Muslim genuinely feels there is a demon in wine which causes the drinker to lapse from good behaviour, Mr Waugh also emphasizes that alcohol was disallowed as it is a diuretic and therefore promotes dehydration and thirst – an undesirable craving to have in the desert. As one mother expressed it when confronted by her student son, home from the university, looking aghast at the breakfast bacon and eggs and finishing off the teapot, 'I cannot think what keeps my son out so late at night. It cannot be drinking, as he is always so thirsty in the morning.'

The influence of alcohol on the psyche is as important as its influence on the physique. Its ability to loosen inhibitions – although rightly condemned if the resulting behaviour is anti-social – has considerable advantages. Alcohol enables the shy to communicate with ease and the tense to relax; it is this tranquillizing effect which has made it a desirable part of any celebratory occasion by allowing us to be our natural selves.

Modern life brings with it such extreme stresses that the benefits of modest drinking are obvious (as unfortunately are the temptations to over-indulge). For many people, the daily grind starts with a difficult journey to work in the morning and continues relentlessly until they are home again in the evening. Even the comparative security of home surroundings are not without their own pressures: family life is harder, tougher and not as comforting as it was a generation ago.

A drink when the weary worker returns home may afford him or her the opportunity to readapt to the different environment. Research has shown that the times when stress is maximal are when the worker first reaches the office or factory and when he or she returns home. Not to be able to sit down and think about the day in the office before being confronted with its problems reinforces the trouble. Likewise, on reaching home, a short time alone to sort out one's thoughts before discussing domestic matters is a great stress reliever. At this time a modest drink may relax the overwrought system, thereby allaying the psychosomatic diseases – some potentially dangerous and all

"HE IS MUCH LESS SHY AFTER HIS SECOND GLASS"

inconvenient – which can attack the organs of the body.

Alcohol was drunk for thousands of years before the birth of Christ. Its effects have always excited comment – the first condemnation of over-indulgence was recorded in 3,000 BC. Tennessee Williams understood the allure of drinking, and frequently explained how he always needed to drink until he felt 'the click'. Williams's 'click' is the point at which one feels relaxed and at ease with the world. Since I came across the phrase I must have talked to hundreds of people who have been concerned about their need for drink and who can all recognize the point when their evening drink achieves this objective. The danger of relying on this support is increasingly acknowledged; patients are aware of how easy it would be to go beyond this point if life became difficult.

The Methodists, and the temperance movement in general, are not only concerned about the long-term effect of alcohol on the physical and mental health of those who drink, but also its disinhibitory effects. They feel that the sorrow it creates for the minority who drink to excess is so great that the majority, for whom it only increases happiness, should forgo the pleasures it has to offer. The nineteenth century was particularly concerned at the fact that alcohol blunted the conscience and released anger as well as allowing the libido to run unchecked. In this, the advocates of temperance were perpetuating a misogynistic tradition. Medieval carvings in churches depict woman as the Temptress, luring man to vice and everlasting damnation in the flames of hell, rather than man as the aggressor. Initially the Methodists' great fear of public houses was not because of the beer sold there, but the chance that women of doubtful reputation, who lurked around bars, might tempt members of their congregation.

Thackeray did not always think of woman as the Temptress, but sometimes as possible prey. In his *Paris Sketchbook*, a not infrequent male approach is honestly admitted:

> You know my way with the women; champagne's the thing; make 'em drink, make 'em talk – make 'em talk, make 'em do anything.

Alcohol does have a disinhibitory effect as well as a tranquillizing one, but in small quantities this can be helpful. Balancing the advantages of drinking reasonable amounts of alcohol against the hazards of excessive drinking is an art which has always attracted attention. People's attempts to achieve this balance often result in comedy or tragedy, but down the millennia most have succeeded in finding the equilibrium which affords them enjoyment and improves their health.

Does this mean that the evening drink after a hard day's work should be condemned? Any answer would have to take into account the increase in overall life expectancy found in light or moderate drinkers, for there is strong circumstantial evidence that part of this is a result of the relaxing properties of alcohol. Studying the effects of alcohol on the human body allows a more informed approach to its power for good or ill. There are very few medical indications for total abstinence: drinking alcohol is not recommended when some medicines have been prescribed. It is now usual for the bottle from the chemist to be labelled with a warning if the pills or tablets would react with alcohol. Some doctors are opposed to the patient taking alcohol if the course of tablets is comparatively short. They fear that the patient may forget to take an essential dose if their memory has been blunted by more than a couple of drinks.

Patients with liver disease, alcoholic cardiomyopathies, some forms of epilepsy or pancreatitis, and those who are alcoholics should avoid even the occasional drink. Many forms of indigestion, including reflux oesophagitis (heartburn), are exacerbated by alcohol, and these patients may also find that they suffer from a husky voice the next day. This is not a definitive list, but most people are healthy and a drink is more likely to do good than harm.

1

A brief history of alcohol

Of all drinks, wine is most profitable, of medicines most pleasant, and of dainty viands most harmless.

When Plutarch wrote these words, grapes had already been cultivated for thousands of years and wine had been drunk for even longer. Vines have been on the earth for some two million years, but it is only in the last ten thousand that, thanks to man's intervention, they have produced grapes sufficiently juicy to provide the wine that has since played a pivotal role in our lives. There are now 24,000 varieties of vine known to botanists, but only ninety are of much interest to the vineyard owner – and of these, only sixteen are classified as 'classic' vines, such as Cabernet Sauvignon, Chardonnay, Riesling and Pinot Noir. The actual cultivar may vary from country to country, as different clones have been developed to suit the local environment and even the microclimate of the vineyard.

The joys of drinking fermented grapes had been recorded in Assyria before 10,000 BC and, at the same time, other grains and fruits had been used in the production of fermented drinks. Beer too had its origins in Assyria, although no one knows the exact date. Cereals were first cultivated in 6,000 BC, and by 3,000 BC the Sumerian poet had written:

> I feel wonderful, drinking beer in a blissful mood
> with joy in my heart, and a happy liver.

Beer was so highly valued that its local name was *kash*, which survives even today as 'cash'. It was used for bartering and to pay wages, not only of the manual labourers but also of those in authority, such as the administrators who worked for the ruling family. By the time of the Pharaohs brewing was big business in Egypt, and beer was produced in many different grades: the aristocracy and the high officials preferred their beer dark and old, whereas the manual labourers were given it when still young and pale.

In ancient Egypt and Mesopotamia beer was made by the simple method of combining barley and water, allowing it to ferment and then adding leaves, and later dates or honey, to flavour it, in the same way as hops are used today. Although hops seem to be so essential to the flavour of beer, they were in fact only introduced to England in the fifteenth century. The practice took some time to become established, as to many the hop was a 'pernicious weed'; Norwich led the opposition by outlawing beer which was made with it, and Henry VIII forbade the use of hops in any beer drunk at Court.

In China as long ago as 4,500 BC, district leaders enjoyed their rice wine out of exquisitely carved jugs, examples of which can be found in the British Museum. In 1996, an edict from China's prime minister Li Peng demanded that wine rather than spirits be served at all ministerial receptions, as it more closely represents Chinese culture and its 'ethical progress'.

At the same time as the Chinese established a ritual for their drinking, the indigenous inhabitants of the Americas had also developed their own alcoholic drinks, but made from honey and maize rather than rice. So firmly is western Europe established in people's minds as the centre of viticulture and viniculture that it is hard to believe that the wines of Chile, which have been skilfully made since the sixteenth century, are still referred to as new wines. The vineyards of western Europe, first established around 2,500 BC, are themselves relatively new compared with those which were planted in 5,000 BC in Syria and parts of Palestine. Although the vines were not grown in what we today would recognize as vineyards, wine was first deliberately made, and viticulture established, in the villages between the Caspian and the Black Sea.

Appropriately for a race which coined the word 'democracy', it was only when the Greeks established their vineyards that wine became a pleasure available to everyone, regardless of their class. Drinking wine had first become a custom amongst the ruling classes of the Assyrian Empire in the first millennium BC. These ancient vineyards provided reasonable wine, and drinking it was a privilege jealously guarded by the élite. Beer made from barley was the alcoholic drink most usually enjoyed by the masses. In ancient Egypt, as in Babylon, what was drunk depended on the prosperity and power of the drinker: fermented dates, rather than barley, were the basis of the drink made available to the toiling classes. Even many of the people important enough to figure around 1,500 BC in the pictures of bawdy wine-drinking found in the tombs were probably drinking wine made from dates. Conversely, various works of art from this period show the ancient Egyptian nobility drinking the more desirable grape wine.

There are Egyptian tomb paintings which illustrate the whole process of wine making and are readily interpreted by anyone conversant with modern viticulture. The ritual of serving wine at the patrician banqueting table had sexual connotations; ancient Egyptian culture reflected the fact that alcohol is intimately related to other pleasures of the flesh. At the banquets the women were revealingly clad, those who served the wine wore erotic symbols, and it is interesting that the hieroglyph for pouring wine is the same as that for ejaculating.

The ancient civilizations had their wine buffs who were every bit as enthusiastic and knowledgeable as their latter-day successors. Taking an 'aesthetic interest' (as it is described in the Napa Valley) in wine drinking is no new phenomenon. Many of the classical philosophers and writers who made Latin and Greek such misery for generations of students also wrote about wine, and on occasions may have been inspired by it. The well-known but anonymous lines:

> Aristotle, that master of arts,
> Had been but a dunce without wine
> And what we ascribe to his parts,
> Is but due to the juice of the vine.

describe the feelings of some nineteenth-century scholar. Whereas Hippocrates and Galen analysed the medicinal value of wine, Pliny and Strabo were as much the specialized wine writers of their time as those who write in the Sunday supplements of today. They particularly enjoyed wine from Kos (which would have pleased Hippocrates), Lesbos and Chios, but rejected that from other Greek islands as being of inferior quality. They commented not only on the palatability of wines from different vineyards and regions, but also, like some elderly London clubman, gave an opinion on their likely development.

Slaves in Rome were given a handsome daily allowance of wine to inspire them to work and inure them to their plight. Similarly, the ability of Roman soldiers to survive the rigours and diseases of their conquering marches was partly attributed to their wine ration. During the latter centuries of the Roman occupation wine was no longer keeping, because of changes in the nature of the containers, and had to be drunk much younger. This may have enhanced its medicinal powers, for a wine in which all the tannin has been oxidized by the passage of time contains less of the efficacious flavonoids.

By AD 100, Roman writers were comparing different wines and vintages in as much detail, given the constraints of the time, as a twentieth-century wine merchant's catalogue. Then, as now, it was important that a vintage should be drunk when the wine was at its best; wine could be stored in amphorae for a number of years, thus allowing it to mature.

The advent of barrels in the second century AD was the beginning of the end of laying down wine so that it could improve by keeping; the practice only became possible once more with the re-introduction of glass bottles. Though they had been used in Roman times, bottles only became available again in the twelfth century, and were not reintroduced on a grand scale until the seventeenth century. Even then, until the end of that century the bottles were not used for long-term storage but merely as decanters. In his book *Wine Snobbery* Andrew Barr suggests that until the seventeenth century the glass from which bottles were made was too fragile to allow wine to be stored, and they tended to break if an attempt was made to cork them. In the seventeenth century Chianti bottles were wrapped in straw to protect them when the wine was being moved; the woven straw covering which made the Chianti bottle such a popular interior decoration feature in the 1960s is a vestige from this period.

Once lead crystal became available in the late seventeenth century, the bottle necks could be made strong enough to take a good cork and were not so easily broken when stored in the cellar. Andrew Barr emphasizes that it is no coincidence that Ravenscroft introduced lead crystal glass at the same time as champagne was pioneered in France. Had it not been for lead crystal, champagne would never have been possible: it is too subtle a wine to be kept in casks, and the pressure from the carbon dioxide it contains would have shattered the old-style bottle, even had it been possible to fit a champagne cork into it. Now there was a demand for cork, the techniques used for its production started to improve and it soon became possible to store wine in glass bottles. Without these advances, we would never have had the pleasure of going into a cellar and seeing rows of port, claret and champagne bottles, and these wines would never have become an integral part of British culture.

The first evidence of vineyards in the Holy Land was discovered in Jericho and dates from 5,000 BC. As alcohol has played such an important part in the history of the Mediterranean region, it is little wonder that the Bible contains so many references to wine. As the Old Testament gives way to the New Testament, so does disapproval give way to approval. In the New Testament, wine figures in the parables, the history and above all, of course, in the ritual. Timothy, like Hippocrates, had no doubt about wine's good qualities. Many a traditional parson has had reason to be grateful to 1 Timothy 5:23, which gives the clergy scriptural permission to keep a good cellar and to enjoy its contents:

> Drink no longer water, but use a little wine for thy stomach's sake and thine often infirmities.

There is a popular belief that, once the civilizing influence of the Roman Empire ended, so did the cultivation of vineyards in western Europe and with it the enjoyment of wine. But viticulture was maintained in both secular and ecclesiastical life. The Romans while in Britain had planted vineyards, and these continued to yield after they had left; it is known that by the ninth century many were flourishing in southern England. The Norman invasion of the eleventh century did more than just introduce the manners and language of the French aristocracy to Britain: it stimulated wine growing, causing a great increase in the number of vineyards. By the time of the Domesday Book of 1086, they were recorded as far north as Ely, and there were several in the London area.

The Normans did not, however, extinguish the breweries that were prospering at the time of the invasion, as they concluded that beer was already too established a part of English culture to be entirely replaced by wine. In the eighth century, for example, the church decreed that English monks should be allowed up to eight pints of beer a day. Although the beer was very weak, it probably meant that vespers was sung with great gusto.

The Normans laid down rules for brewing beer and penalties for brewers whose standards were inadequate. The English monasteries were as proud of their breweries as their French counterparts were of their vineyards. Thomas à Becket was a brewer as well as a churchman, and consequently a discerning judge of beer. Roger Protz's book *The Ale Trail* recounts how Becket went to France with two cartloads of beer as a present for the French diplomats. The French were amazed at British beer, describing it as:

A drink most wholesome, clear of all dregs, rivalling wine in colour and surpassing it in flavour.

The French may have expressed amazement, but they also had their own breweries. The English were far from being the only Europeans to have refined the art of brewing: in Germany alone there were between four and five hundred monasteries with well-established breweries, each inordinately proud of its output. Every European country had its distinctive beers, just as they do now.

Within a hundred years of the Norman invasion, trading with the Continent had become relatively easy and British tastes in wine, as in other things, had become more sophisticated. Home-grown wine was spurned, perhaps wisely, and the British transferred their custom to the wine growers of France and later Portugal. On the Continent the increasing demand for wine resulted in the need for the estates of the church and other landowners to produce enough for sale as well as for local consumption. The demand for wine was not only spreading northwards to France and Britain, but also to Scandinavia and Russia. There was a brisk wine trade in the Eastern Mediterranean, spreading from Turkey up through the Black Sea and along the great waterways of the Balkans and Russia.

The European export market prompted the development of specialist regional wines. The growers in each region began to produce an individual wine derived from specific grapes that had been cultivated to fill a perceived gap in the overall market. Both Pinot Noir and Gamay have, for instance, been cultivated in Burgundy since the 1300s, although as in other areas, wines are also made from other grapes for local consumption. Before this development, varieties of vine had been planted at the whim of the local landowner. The resulting wine was of variable type and its quality from year to year was very inconsistent.

As the market for wine has grown, so the system of wine making has had to change. Each period of expansion in the wine trade can be related to the availability and cost of the labour needed to cultivate the vines and make the wine. The first boom in wine growing was at the time of the Roman Empire, when there was no problem with either the availability or cost of labour as there was a constant supply of slaves. Medieval Europe saw the next great expansion, but fortunately for the future of the wine industry the well-established feudal system furnished all the labour the landowner might need to work his vineyards.

In the last fifty years a global market for good wine has grown up, and demand continues to increase. Labour is now expensive, and in consequence it is cheaper to replace people by machinery. The development of mechanical processes has enabled the huge demand to be met. Not all vineyards have become mechanized, however, and it is reassuring to know that some are still producing wine as it was made 2,000 years ago and are still capable of exciting one's sense of history. As Petronius reported:

Wine lives longer than man . . . for wine is life.

The history of drinking is not just that of wine and beer. Bacchus was as familiar with the products of distillation as he was with those made by the fermentation of grapes and cereals.

Whisky is reputed to have been first made by the ancient Egyptians, who distilled barley. The habit of whisky drinking is thought to have spread from Ireland, and to have been introduced to Scotland by missionary monks. However, there is no evidence that small stills did not already exist in the Highlands, just as they did in Ireland. The first reference to whisky in an official document appears in the Scottish Exchequer Rolls in 1494, and by the end of that century it seems that the drink was well established at all levels of society. Whisky was the preferred drink of the Scottish royal court at this time, and was even used at communion when wine was not available. Scotch and Irish whiskies are still the best in the world.

In the seventeenth century whisky was distilled in many private houses and was sometimes given as part-wage to the agricultural worker. After the Union in 1707 illicit distilling became very popular, and was only partially controlled by the parliamentary act which followed the Royal Commission of 1823. The 1823 Act made it comparatively easy for anyone to distil whisky legally on purchase of a license and payment of a reasonable level of duty. Despite this, illicit distilling continued for many years and even into my own lifetime. Some of the finest whisky I have ever tasted had been distilled in Sutherland and was served from an old medicine bottle.

Although they may have been distilled since the days of the Pharaohs, spirits as we know them today are relative newcomers compared to wine. Initially, Continental spirits were regarded as medicines rather than drinks. So popular were these 'medicines' that they were taken regularly by a large proportion of the population, irrespective of their state of health.

The Dutch, like the British, were trend-setters in the drinking customs of northern Europe. Credit for first distilling brandy from French wine should go to the late seventeenth-century wine merchants of the Netherlands; the link with Holland is forever commemorated by the word 'brandy', a corruption of the Dutch word *brandewijn*, which means 'burnt wine'. Until the 1914–18 war, brandy had greater social cachet as a drink than whisky, despite the latter's very much longer history. But during the First World War whisky became the spirit preferred by the army and has never looked back. Even now, however, between 15 and 20 per cent of all of the Scotch whisky sold in Britain is consumed in Scotland.

In Elizabethan times sherry was one of the most popular wines in England. Its popularity faded in the late seventeenth century, but it enjoyed a resurgence in the second half of the nineteenth century and the first half of the twentieth.

It is arguable that, for more than three hundred years, drinking in the more traditional places, such as embassies, clubs and officers' messes, as well as private dining rooms, has revolved around the same trinity of wines: champagne, claret and port. At the time of Pepys claret was still imported in the cask; he describes how in 1663 he had a thoroughly good morning's drinking as he shared some Haut Brion (which Pepys renders as 'Ho Bryan') with Sir J. Cutler and Mr Grant at the Royall Oake Taverne in Lombard Street. Pepys had quite a liking for Haut Brion, which he described as having a

. . . good and most particular taste but I never met with . . .

Wine imported in the cask inevitably oxidized, but later that century, when lead crystal glass became available and corks could be fitted, vintages could be kept. The cult of the vintage wine and the private cellar became re-established.

Champagne became popular in Britain as a result of the considerable French influence at the court of Charles II. Its success might even have been a reflection of the choice of Louise de Kérouaille, later Duchess of Portsmouth, as Charles's favourite mistress.

In France itself, surprisingly, champagne did not become established as a favoured drink at court until the following century. There has always been a story that the shape of Marie Antoinette's curvaceous breasts influenced the traditional design of the champagne glass, although this has always seemed most unlikely. Enthusiasts have usually preferred to drink champagne out of a fluted glass, and some very elegant eighteenth-century glasses illustrate this. Whatever the reasons for the introduction of champagne and however it is drunk, Joseph d'Argent, a French wine merchant, summed up its role:

No government could survive without champagne. Champagne in the throats of our diplomatic people is like oil in the wheels of an engine. Burgundy for kings, champagne for duchesses and claret for gentlemen.

As there have always been far more gentlemen than kings or duchesses in Britain, it is not surprising that claret has been the mainstay of British wine drinkers. Wines have been imported from Bordeaux for centuries, but the trade declined in the fifteenth century, only to be revived in the second half of the seventeenth century, at the same time as champagne was introduced. This revitalized trade was once again blighted when war broke out between France and England; the Bordeaux wine producers and shippers were hard-hit by the import taxes that limited English demand.

Port, which completes the trinity, also became a popular drink in the latter part of the seventeenth century. The war between England and France which so devastated the Bordeaux trade provided an opportunity for the Portuguese to increase their share of the market, and in 1703 the Methuen Treaty between Portugal and England decisively sealed a partnership between the port growers and shippers in Portugal and the English drinking public. This association, originally foisted on the British people by politics and differential taxation caused by war, became firmly established and still continues. The descendants of some of the original British settlers in Oporto are still trading today.

For most people, alcohol in moderation is more likely to improve rather than damage their health. Because alcohol is dangerous in excess, its advantages are often overlooked.

Set yourself a limit before you start an evening's drinking.

Try to keep track of when and what you drink.

Avoid drinking on an empty stomach.

It is better to drink at meal times, or at any rate with some food. Snacks should be served when drinks are offered.

Be aware of the difficulties of measuring a drink when pouring one at home. Most home-poured gins and whiskies are at least double the tot provided by the local publican (see table on p. 9).

Drink slowly, and dilute spirits with at least as much water. This might shock the Scots but it would help their health.

2

Antioxidants and flavonoids

The ancients hoped to preserve their health by balancing the Four Humours: choler, black bile, phlegm and blood. Hippocrates, who lived in Kos between about 460 and 370 BC, was convinced that the judicious use of wine could stimulate these humours if they were flagging, and restore them if they were depleted. Two and a half thousand years later, doctors are still recommending wine for its medicinal qualities.

All alcohol improves most people's health when taken in moderation, but red wine seems to have a very special quality. Hippocrates never gave any indication he understood that the seat of wine's pharmaceutical power lay in the skin of the grapes, the pips, and possibly even the stalks. However, another ancient, Pliny the Elder, whether by chance or observation, hit upon the truth that the skin of the grapes, the vine shoots, the leaves and pips all had medicinal uses. Pliny regarded wine as a panacea:

Wine in itself is a remedy, it nourishes the blood of man,
it delights the stomach and soothes care and affliction.

Red wine and some of the darker beers owe part of their health-promoting powers to a group of chemicals they contain, the flavonoids and other antioxidants. Medical endorsement of the half-bottle of red wine each day has been reassuring, but the average claret drinker does not need his doctor to help him to order his wine. His own experience, and that of his peers, has shown him that two to four drinks a day has helped him to stay fit and has improved his sense of physical and mental well-being.

Although medicine has become rather more complicated over the last few thousand years and today we have greater knowledge of the ills that can affect us, many of the old remedies still

31

have their place. All that has changed is that now we are more often able to say what makes them so effective.

The advantages of drinking red wine have received so much

" IRONIC INNIT – WE JUST GET USED TO RED WINE WHEN WE READ THAT DARK BEER'S GOOD FOR US AFTER ALL"

recent publicity that it might appear that other forms of alcoholic drink have no value. This is not so. The elderly clubman may derive a greater advantage from drinking red wines, but his contemporary enjoying beer in the George and Dragon may also be prolonging his life. Alcohol has a medicinal value over and above the flavonoids the drink contains. Pliny's comments were two thousand years ahead of their time in their astuteness, but Hippocrates' prescription was not wrong: he just did not know that the skin of the grape is more important than the juice.

Our survival depends on the body's ability to annihilate the thousands of pathogenic (disease-bearing) organisms it is likely to come into contact with every day, and on having an efficient immune system able to counteract malignant disease. Problems brought about by the degenerative conditions which sooner or later are likely to affect us all also have to be overcome.

A damaging process now being understood for the first time is the effect of free radicals on a person's health. The very term 'free radical' may strike terror into the heart of anyone who dreaded science classes at school, but their influence on health is so important that some superficial understanding of their action is necessary.

The good news, which makes studying the function of free radicals so exciting, is that it is the ability of alcohol to counteract them which gives the evening drink some of its medicinal quality. Free radicals are wandering, imperfect atoms which have an unpaired electron always searching for a home. They are highly charged little devils, medical mischief makers, for as atoms circulating with an unpaired electron in the human body they are always seeking another cell to which the lonely electron can become attached. On finding a refuge, the atom's wholeness is restored, but the defect is handed on and the instability spreads.

Once the electron finds the necessary companion, it can start a chain reaction, which in the wrong circumstances can be destructive. The action of free radicals is not always bad, for they help to destroy bacteria, and the oxidation they set up is useful in extracting energy in the metabolic processes that provide nourishment for the cells. But destructive oxidation initiated by the free radicals is responsible for a number of diseases.

Research on free radicals began fifty years ago, but it is only recently that their significance to modern medicine has been understood. Good health may depend on our body's ability to reduce the free radicals in the system by limiting the number produced. This may be achieved by antioxidants, substances which inhibit the oxidation processes initiated by free radicals.

The problems arise when there are too many free radicals circulating and not enough partners with whom they can link. An abnormal oxidation process has been shown to be instrumental in the formation of atheroma – the sticky, porridge-like material

which blocks our arteries as we grow older – and has been implicated in such diverse diseases as cataracts, macular degeneration
of the retina, the cause of much of the blindness of old age, and
very possibly in the development of cancers and other malignant
diseases.

Detailed knowledge of free radicals is fortunately not necessary for us to appreciate that any food or drink which contains
antioxidants, the antidotes to free radicals, may postpone the day
when our arteries fur up with atheroma. If serious atheroma
develops in coronary arteries, a cold winter afternoon's walk
may be interrupted as the walker experiences the gripping pain
of angina. In even less fortunate people, the free radicals may
lead to one of their organs falling prey to malignant change.

Flavonoids are found in a wide variety of fresh foodstuffs.
Many fruits and vegetables are rich in them, so one of the
answers to the problems created by free radicals lies in our gar-
dens if we live in the country, and on the greengrocer's stall if our
habitat is the town. These are not the only source of antioxidants.
For those who enjoy a drink, whether they live in the town or the
country, some of the solution to aberrant oxidation rests in the
wine cellar, in the beer barrel and the whisky decanter.

A bag of carrots or onions, a bottle of wine, a pint of dark beer
and a clove of garlic all contain potent antioxidants: the
flavonoids. If the food we eat or drink is rich in flavonoids, this
may deal with the oxidation initiated by the marauding free radicals. There are more than three thousand known flavonoids
found in common foodstuffs, notably in onions, garlic, fruit and
vegetable skins in general, apples, red wine, dark beer and tea.

Vitamin C is also a potent antioxidant, and its beneficial effect
on the incidence of coronary heart disease has recently been documented. It appears to be especially important for men.

Tea drinkers also have high levels of flavonoids in their diet.
The average British tea drinker takes four cups a day – only the
Australians have a higher intake. Tea is also rich in folates, and
so, contrary to popular belief, a steady intake of tea when pregnant is likely to be beneficial, and will supplement the folic acid

tablets the mother should already be taking. An occasional glass of burgundy or claret accompanying plain English cooking will provide additional flavonoids.

The health problems which beset people living in some parts of Scotland provide a terrible warning to those who do not understand the value of antioxidants, in this case those found in vegetables. As we have seen, in districts where it is customary to have a diet rich in vegetables, the incidence of coronary heart disease is comparatively low. But in south-west Scotland it is higher than almost anywhere else in the world. This has been partly attributed to the inhabitants' scorn of green vegetables and love of chips. It is a myth that only the poorer areas of Glasgow have a large number of chip shops; they are almost as common in the West End of Glasgow as in the Southside. The problem is not confined to Glasgow, however: throughout Scotland the incidence of coronary heart disease has been related to the lack of enthusiasm for vegetables.

In most places in Scotland the favourite drink of the younger generation is beer, whereas those who are older drink large amounts of whisky. Wine drinking is increasing, but has not yet achieved the popularity it has in England. If Scottish drinking patterns were to change so that red wine played a greater part, if the Scots ate more vegetables and smoked less, the incidence of heart disease might show some improvement.

Professor Tom Whitehead of Birmingham University has said that flavonoids are both ubiquitous and powerful, perhaps more effective as antioxidants than vitamins C and E and beta-carotene, which were initially thought to be the most powerful antioxidants available in the diet. Beta-carotene is a precursor of vitamin A, and is particularly useful as a dietary supplement as, unlike vitamin A, it is not likely to cause serious trouble in over-dose. Too much beta-carotene will colour the soles of the feet and the palms of the hands yellow and will even affect the general complexion, but it does no lasting damage.

Professor Whitehead and others have been studying the flavonoids in wine and have confirmed that they are more abundant in red wine than in other drinks. Recent research confirms that some dark beers, such as Guinness and other stouts, also contain flavonoids.

The concentration of flavonoids varies from one wine to another. They are present in greater quantities in red wines because the techniques used involve the retention of the grape skins for very much longer and this is a significant part of the vinification process. Conversely, when white wine is made the grape skins, with their quota of health-giving flavonoids, are removed early in the vinification and the bottle of wine, the final product, is deprived of its antioxidant powers. Although white wine does not contain a clinically significant amount of flavonoids, it has, in common with all alcoholic drinks, cardio-protective powers derived from other sources.

Wine has the advantage of being a natural foodstuff. Although scientific interest is now concentrating on the flavonoids, other antioxidants – including a host of carotenoids – are also of great medical significance. Carotenoids are also found in the yellow and orange fruits and vegetables, such as carrots, apricots and peppers, and also in the darker green vegetables such as broccoli and green beans. As we have seen, the antioxidants also include vitamin C, E and beta carotene, and the interaction of these vitamins with flavonoids may be an important part of the antioxidant reaction, giving a clue as to why drinking with meals may be of particular dietary benefit.

Many of the carotenoids found in fresh fruit and vegetables have not yet been fully evaluated. It does seem, however, with the benefit of knowledge gleaned from population studies, that until more is known about carotenoids and flavonoids, and their isolation has been perfected, a diet rich in fruit and vegetables accompanied by wine is likely to be better for us than swallowing handfuls of vitamin pills.

Pills containing vitamins and trace elements do have their place in a healthy diet, and taking them is a practice which should not be denigrated. The pace of modern life, particularly as it affects the young office worker battling with life in front of the computer, makes it difficult for them to have the type of lunch enjoyed by their parents' generation. By the time they finally reach home at the end of the day, there is often not enough time to eat properly before moving on to the evening's entertainment. Even at weekends, when there might be time to eat well, it is impossible to ensure that the vegetables on the dinner table are always fresh. Research has shown that in three days, which is the time it takes for most fresh vegetables to make the journey from the farm to the market stall, 50 per cent of the vitamins may be lost. Frozen vegetables retain their vitamin content, but these may not be taken in sufficient variety to provide all the supplements needed to keep the diner healthy.

In some situations, as illustrated by the example of folic acid, no diet can be naturally rich enough in a vitamin for the body to obtain it in sufficient quantities to keep all pathological conditions at bay. The high levels of folic acid needed to prevent many congenital abnormalities in babies can only be achieved if the woman who is pregnant, or hoping to be, takes additional folic acid in tablet form. Similarly, enhanced levels of folic acid are cardio-protective. A recent survey has suggested that high levels of folates in the blood reduce the incidence of coronary heart disease by 40 per cent, another explanation for the reduced likelihood of moderate drinkers having cardiovascular disease.

My own advice to patients is to eat up their greens, to take plenty of fresh fruit and to swallow vitamin supplements as well. Folic acid is only one such supplement that is a useful antioxidant. It is also one of several vitamins that may be in short supply in those who drink, even if their diet is otherwise healthy. Even some patients who are regular, moderate drinkers show evidence of folate deficiency, and most heavy drinkers would benefit from the folic acid supplements which may be bought over the counter at the chemists. This is dealt with in greater detail in Chapters 4 and 5 but, in general, the nursery advice to eat up your greens and the doctors' advice to have an apple a day is still as important in 1997 as it was in 1897.

It is possible to take some vitamins, notably A and D, to excess.

Care must be exercised when taking multi-vitamin preparations that these two are not present in more than one pill, in which case overdosage could readily occur.

To many, half a bottle of red wine is more enjoyable than either vitamin pills or a plateful of broccoli – although this does not excuse omitting vegetables or vitamins from the diet. Some of the flavonoids in red wine have been shown to be up to twenty times more powerful than vitamin E.

The flavonoids which were found first and have therefore been studied in the greatest depth are resveratrol, quercetin, catechin, epicatechin and rutin. Others are constantly being isolated, and new information about those already discovered is regularly published. Different flavonoids occur in varying quantities in grapes, and the amounts are further altered, and their properties changed, by the vinification. The type of grape, the climate in which it ripened, the soil on which the vine is growing and the wine-making process all have to be taken into consideration when assessing a wine's health-enhancing properties.

The most abundant flavonoid found in grapes is catechin. Although more plenteous than other flavonoids and a powerful antioxidant, it is not as useful in preventing the clumping of platelets as some of the others (such as resveratrol). Platelets are the small particles in the blood which are a crucial part of the clotting process. If they are too sticky, the blood is apt to clot readily, and the scene is set for a potentially fatal coronary thrombosis or stroke. Epicatechin has similar properties to catechin.

Quercetin has recently been investigated very thoroughly. It has been shown to be a powerful antioxidant and therefore efficient at reducing atherosclerosis, the accumulation of atheroma which in time can fur up the coronary arteries within the heart and the brain, as well as the arteries which lead to the brain, kidneys and limbs.

Quercetin has also been shown to have anti-carcinogenic properties. A United States National Cancer Institute study found that a high intake of quercetin was associated with a reduced incidence of cancers of the digestive tract. Quercetin is found in reasonable quantities in all grape varieties that have ripened in hot sun.

Resveratrol is the flavonoid which has captured the attention of scientists investigating the value of wine; not only was it isolated before the others, but it has been shown to be a useful marker for the presence of other flavonoids. If any grape has a reasonable resveratrol count, it is a good bet that it will also contain other flavonoids.

Unlike quercetin, resveratrol in grapes is best nurtured in a cool, damp climate. It is therefore more likely to be found in grapes from the more temperate, wetter climes of France than in those grown in vineyards baked by the sun. Cabernet Sauvignon, for instance, has a high resveratrol content in clarets produced in Bordeaux, but when Italian wine is produced from the same grapes the levels are much lower. Resveratrol is not a particularly strong antioxidant, but it is effective in ensuring that the body's cholesterol contains a high proportion of the cardio-protective, high-density lipoprotein cholesterol (HDL).

The benefits of wine drinking are part of the developing story of cholesterol levels and their relation to heart disease. Knowledge about cholesterol has gone beyond the simple belief that all one needs to do to control it is cut back on bacon, eggs, butter, milk and other dairy produce.

The biochemical background to the control of the blood's fat levels is complex, and alcohol intake is one of the factors which influences it. Twenty-five years ago, dinner party guests discussed their cholesterol levels as freely as they did their golf handicaps. The overall level was considered the clue to longevity, but it is now known that this is too simplistic an approach: the amount of low-density lipoprotein (LDL) cholesterol together with the proportion of high-density lipoprotein (HDL) to the total cholesterol gives a better indication of the likelihood of escaping a heart attack.

The science of fat metabolism does not have to be understood in detail, but it is of importance to those who drink alcohol. Any form of alcohol taken in moderation lowers the amount of LDL and increases the proportion of HDL to total cholesterol. HDL cholesterol is probably cardio-protective, whereas a high level of LDL is certainly associated with damage to the arteries, formation of atheroma and cardiovascular disease.

There is also some evidence that a reasonable intake of red wine has a greater beneficial effect on the levels of cholesterol than other drinks. Conversely, a very heavy alcohol intake *increases* the overall cholesterol level together with the quantity of triglyceride, another of the blood fats which has been implicated in the development of heart disease.

Resveratrol prevents cardiac disease not only by helping to ensure that the blood's cholesterol levels are in the right proportions, but by being efficient at reducing platelet stickiness, another factor in the formation of coronary thrombosis. When clumped together, platelets form an important part of the clotting mechanism. A platelet's tendency to clump is affected both by the flavonoids and the ethyl alcohol – both factors are important – and this is one of the reasons why alcoholic drinks other than wine are able to reduce the incidence of thrombosis.

Rutin, also a flavonoid, has recently been isolated from grape skins and would seem to be a strong antioxidant, but more news is awaited.

It is unlikely that wine drinkers will choose a wine from the list because of its influence on the coronary arteries and the platelets; they will rather be tempted by its colour, nose and effect on the palate. However, as the resveratrol count of the grape varies so much from one country to another and from one grape variety to another, it is always interesting to know just how good the half-bottle of wine enjoyed at dinner will be at keeping the coronary blood flowing throughout the 'long, slow watches of the night' and the following day.

Recent research from Sweden has confirmed the widely held view that binge drinking is associated with a significant mortality after the session is over. After the immediate cardio-protective effect has worn off, there is an increased risk of disaster. Some might be surprised to hear that, in so far as the mortality is the result of ischaemic strokes – those which result from the obstruction of a blood vessel in the brain rather than from a cerebral haemorrhage – this increase is absent if the binge drinkers have been drinking red wine: the cardio-protective effect of the red wine more than outweighs the influence of the alcohol on the cardiovascular system.

There is one bit of disappointing news. The older vintage wines, which have been lovingly kept at an even temperature in controlled surroundings, have a lower resveratrol count than they would have if they had been drunk earlier. In order to obtain maximum medicinal advantage from the claret, it needs to be drunk at an age that would be considered infanticide by wine connoisseurs. Maturing wine in oak also reduces the resveratrol count, but even so, it is encouraging to know that the levels in the most distinguished bottle are high enough to help keep our cholesterol in the correct form, our arteries healthy and our platelets from forming lethal clots. Fortified wines, although they have (when taken in moderate amounts) the health-giving properties of all other alcohols, do not have a high flavonoid count.

In general, wines produced by traditional methods are richer in flavonoids than those produced by modern types of vinification. Some of these new techniques are designed to produce a pleasant, immediately drinkable wine, but in achieving a marketable product the flavonoid content has been reduced.

One of the ways in which wine production can be accelerated is to use PVPP, a chemical which artificially lowers the tannin count. If the wine is left to its own devices, this takes years to dissipate, but as a result of PVPP, even quite young wines lose their harshness and bitterness. Unfortunately, the method does not only reduce the tannin – which anyway is of interest to the wine connoisseur – but also the flavonoids, which worries the doctors. Furthermore, many of the modern wine makers who use PVPP in their wineries are working in areas where the sun is hot and the resveratrol count naturally low.

Early research on flavonoid levels from America was misleading, as it suggested there was no marked difference between the cardio-protective effect of red and white wines. This false trail may well have been laid because the red wine studied had been made in a way which drastically reduced the flavonoid level. Later studies of Californian wines which have taken account of this factor have shown a similar disparity between the cardio-protective power of wines to that displayed in other parts of the world.

The annual race to serve Beaujolais Nouveau may provide amusement for the drinkers and a useful source of revenue for the wine merchants. Unfortunately, in order to make the wine drinkable in the autumn of the same year as the grapes were picked, it has to be specially treated to reduce the tannin, which in turn reduces the flavonoid content. Beaujolais Nouveau is a light, fresh wine, and those who are not too snobbish about it enjoy the yearly ritual of its début on the dinner tables. Drinking the Nouveau will help the health of the arteries, but as its flavonoid count has been sadly depleted, a bottle of Beaujolais Villages, which has been prepared unhurriedly, would have served them even better.

The British are fortunate in that their traditionally favourite wines are also those which are best for their health. The burgundies, clarets, Beaujolais and Rhône valley wines are all rich in flavonoids. Burgundies seem to fare best, for Pinot Noir, the grape universally used to make red burgundy, is rich in resveratrol. Nothing in the natural world is consistent, however, and there are marked regional variations in the quantity and type of flavonoids found in red wines, even when made from the same grape variety: furthermore, microclimates that offer a favourable environment for the development of flavonoids are found in the vineyards of many countries other than France.

Wines from central and south-western France, Switzerland and Canada have all been grown in districts where the climate favours the production of resveratrol. In Italy and Spain, the climate in general is less conducive, but it is never possible to be dogmatic about this, as what matters is the microclimate. In parts of Spain, for instance, although the overall climate is hot and baking, there are small valleys where the atmosphere in summer is suitably cool, damp and conducive to fungus growth, and hence to the making of a wine rich in resveratrol.

It is probable that not all the flavonoids present in grape skins have yet been discovered. This may account for statistics that show the coronary thrombosis rate in Italy as one of the lowest in the world. These figures are a good indication that, even when resveratrol levels are low, other flavonoids may be present in compensatory greater quantities and the rest of the diet taken with the wine may enhance its value.

Balkan wines tend to use grape varieties rich in flavonoids, and as one would expect, this is reflected in the wines from those countries. In many hot New World countries the Pinot Noir grape has been replaced with Pinotage; in consequence, despite the blistering sun the wines may often have a higher resveratrol count than those made of Pinot Noir in, for instance, Italy and Spain. South African wines are particularly health-giving and have high flavonoid counts. Chilean reds are interesting as they show wide variation in the resveratrol count; some have very low levels, but this does not exclude the possibility that other flavonoids may be present with equally cardio-protective powers.

Finally, no one should disparage the cardio-protective advantages of white wines. These may not be as great as those derived from drinking red, but a quarter of a loaf is better than none.

Research into flavonoids in alcoholic drinks, an exciting and surprising aspect of preventative medicine, is still in its infancy. We understand in part why Bordeaux is so good for the arteries, but it is perfectly possible that within a few years similar advantages may be detected in other red wines which, for the moment, do not seem to match Bordeaux's medicinal qualities.

3

The heart

Doctors have been prescribing alcohol for thousands of years. It was, for instance, only within the last thirty years that National Health Service patients in hospital were no longer offered a bottle of beer every day should they so desire. Even twenty-five years ago, Sister kept a ward bottle of brandy in her office and dispensed it not only to patients and their grieving relatives, but also to the junior doctors if they had had a particularly disturbed night. After the consultant's ward round each morning, he would ask Sister who had been up during the night, and those who had were rewarded with a brandy in their coffee: a relaxed approach to alcohol which has disappeared from hospitals, just as it has from nearly all other work places, because fear of over-indulgence dominates policy.

The benefits of alcohol may have lacked the scientific evidence that would convince today's sceptics, but all the proof the old-fashioned physicians needed was to watch the effect on those patients who had two or three drinks a day. They had fewer illnesses, were more alert in old age and had shorter periods of convalescence than those who were either abstainers or heavy drinkers.

Dr William Buchan, fellow of the Royal College of Physicians of Edinburgh in the eighteenth century, wrote a book called *The Family Physician*, even the title of which was in advance of contemporary medical thinking. In some other ways, however, Dr Buchan was a traditional Georgian doctor, so it is interesting to see that his views on alcohol, like the title of his book, so closely reflect present-day opinion. His advice was that a good wine, a well-prepared beer or carefully distilled spirits taken in moderation are beneficial, and only become damaging if they are drunk to excess. Dr Buchan's words could be used to support one of the fashionable campaigns to encourage sensible drinking:

Fermented liquors still continue to be the common drink of almost every person who can afford them. We [presumably Dr Buchan's fellow doctors] should rather endeavour to assist people in their choice of their liquors, than pretend to condemn what custom has so firmly established. It is not the moderate use of fermented liquors that hurts mankind; it is excess or using such that are ill-prepared or vitiated.

Later in his chapter on drinking, Dr Buchan renews his warning about the advantages of drinking being confined to those who drink reasonably and choose well-made liquor:

But while they are ill-prepared, various ways adulterated or taken in excess they [the fermented liquors] must have many pernicious effects.

Dr Buchan was not aware that the reason why those of his patients who drank in moderation lived longer was that their cardiovascular systems, their hearts and their blood vessels were healthier and aged less fast than did those of their abstemious contemporaries.

Nor was I aware when I joined my family's practice in rural Norfolk why there were patients alive and active who would long since have died had they been living in London when I worked there. My experience of rural medicine was gained before doctors had access to the armoury of drugs now available to treat blood pressure, heart failure and coronary arterial occlusion (blockage). The conundrum of their survival puzzled me for a long while, but I slowly realized that there were three components to it.

The patients, now elderly, had taken steady, regular exercise all their lives while working on the land, and indeed despised those who depended on the car. Many of those who had worked on farms had osteoarthritis after years of toiling in windswept, damp fields, and consequently took aspirin daily, which helps to protect the heart and blood vessels. The third factor was that very few of my Norfolk patients were teetotallers.

Wine drinking was not then popular in Norfolk, although those who lived in my practice occasionally drank home-made wines, but they regularly enjoyed their beer and had whisky when there was anything to celebrate. One neighbouring retired farmer took his dog for a walk each morning and then spent the rest of the day leaning against the gate chatting to passers-by. He must have weighed twenty stone and had high blood pressure and a puce complexion. Each day I greeted him as I drove past his gate and each day I was surprised that his maker had spared him for yet another twenty-four hours. His wife was of similar build.

Years later, long after I had left the district, I went back to my old house, and there by the neighbouring gate was the same old man with his wife. Neither seemed to have changed. The farmer invited me in, and over a few drinks we discussed his rheumatism, his blood pressure and his general health. Although there was now treatment for his blood pressure, which he took regularly, I told him that on no account was he to stop either his daily pint or the aspirin mixture. Interestingly, their son was a twentieth-century farmer who drove everywhere in his Jaguar and only took exercise when he went skiing in the winter or to the south of France in the summer. He had married a teetotaller, stopped drinking himself and sadly died of a coronary thrombosis in his early forties. It may have been chance, but if he had taken rather more brisk (but not violent) exercise, if he had lost weight, taken his daily aspirin and not become a teetotaller, he might have lived as long as his father and not succumbed to heart disease in the same way as do so many of my overworked City of London patients.

Dr Buchan's opinion on alcohol is now the standard medical view. Over the last fifty years, however, it has sometimes been difficult to support his commonsense approach against the advocates of the better-documented healing powers of modern medicine and the prejudice of doctors who have allowed their judgement to be warped by the strain of treating those suffering the ill-effects of heavy drinking.

Although evidence of the benefits of alcohol had been accumulating since the early 1970s it continued to be denied by many doctors until October 1991: an important date, for it was when Sir Richard Doll, the Oxford-based epidemiologist, delivered a paper on the subject. Sir Richard, who produced the evidence that linked cigarette smoking to lung cancer, is internationally accepted as the leader in his field, and when in his paper he endorsed the case for a moderate wine intake, it became medically respectable. Doctors could now discuss the subject with their patients with a clear conscience, and the braver ones could even suggest that they drink wine in moderation.

Even the US Bureau of Alcohol, Tobacco and Firearms now agrees that the label on wine bottles may state that current evidence suggests moderate drinking is associated with a lower risk of coronary heart disease in some individuals. The title of the Bureau is perhaps significant: its combination of duties illustrates the official US view on drinking by linking it with such dangerous pursuits as smoking and the possession of weapons.

The Bureau, however, rejected the suggestion that the label should read: 'There is significant evidence that moderate consumption of alcoholic beverages may reduce the risk of coronary heart disease'. This rejection was not based on the belief that the information was untrue; rather, the Bureau forbade the distribution of additional information recommending moderate drinking on the grounds that it finds 'even truthful statements to be misleading'. This is using the term 'misleading' in the archaic sense of leading its readers away from the paths of righteousness – and therefore presumably in some cases to heavy drinking. By its own admission, the Bureau is not using the word in its modern sense of 'mistaken', and so appears to be making a political comment, to be indulging in social engineering, rather than giving a scientific opinion.

When Sir Richard Doll said that drinking up to four glasses of wine a day reduced the likelihood of coronary thrombosis, he

provided official recognition of the case for moderate alcohol consumption. All those who had advocated this, and had been derided for it, were vindicated.

As is so often the case in medicine, and in science generally, discoveries are made almost simultaneously in different countries. Since the early 1970s rumours had been circulating that French doctors had confirmed that wine had a cardio-protective effect and that this was not shared equally by other forms of alcohol.

At first British doctors dismissed, even ridiculed, the idea that wine could have a greater benefit than other drinks. The cynics suspected that the research was just another example of French commercialism, and that science was being called to the aid of – or possibly even duped by – the vineyards and the wine industry. However, at about the same time doctors in America were showing that moderate drinkers had less heart disease than either teetotallers or heavy drinkers.

Doctor Alan Bailey, working in London, found when analysing the death certificates of predominantly middle-class people that abstainers fared less well than moderate drinkers, and furthermore that although heavy drinkers – defined as those consuming 70 units a week or more – suffered more ill health and died younger from a wider variety of causes, they had less heart disease.

In 1978 Dr Selwyn St Leger, a name now revered by all champions of the 'two to four units a day of alcohol' school of medicine, was working for the Medical Research Council investigating the possible causes of coronary heart disease. After looking at a great many different factors, Dr St Leger came to the conclusion that wine drinking was highly significant in the protection of the coronary arteries, and that wine was superior to other forms of alcoholic drink in this respect. Unwittingly, Dr St Leger had independently supported the work of the French by showing that their claims were not based on a desire to enhance the trade of France's vineyards but on sound scientific observation.

Despite the results of several long-term studies which all showed that moderate drinkers had the lowest mortality – lower either than for heavy drinkers or teetotallers – and the research of Dr St Leger in Cardiff, Dr Klatsky in the USA, Dr Serge Renaud in France and Professor Tom Whitehead in Birmingham (amongst others), the advantages of social drinking were largely ignored.

Two studies in particular produced evidence which no unprejudiced clinician should have disregarded. In California, a research team reviewed the past and present drinking habits of 87,526 female nurses whose life-styles were being studied in detail. The survey showed there was a marked reduction in heart disease in moderate drinkers which far outweighed any increase in death from other causes. Further work with the nurses since the original paper was produced has demonstrated that all-cause mortality is also reduced: moderate drinkers not only have less lethal heart disease but also suffer from fewer other fatal illnesses.

The other ground-breaking study looked at 1,422 male civil servants. These were followed for ten years, and once again light and moderate drinkers showed less evidence of heart disease than did either heavy drinkers or abstainers. All the research demonstrated the same J-shaped curve on the graph plotting the incidence of heart disease against alcohol consumption. Those whose intake placed them at the base of the curve of the J had the fewest heart troubles; the non-drinkers, whose position was on the shorter arm of the J, obviously fared better than the heavy drinkers, who were on the longer arm of the J, but not as well as the moderates.

The reasons why heavy drinkers – those who have more than six drinks a day – develop heart disease are multifarious, but even so, the coronary blood vessels of those who died young were remarkably free of atheroma. This unexpected finding was first noted by pathologists forty or fifty years ago, and Dr Alan Bailey's later research into death certificates confirmed this long-established anecdotal evidence.

Notwithstanding this, and for a variety of reasons, the cardio-vascular system *can* be affected by an excessive alcohol intake, particularly if the drinker also smokes. The effect of smoking is not entirely compensated for by drinking: many heavy smokers who also drink moderately die from coronary heart disease.

I remember two large, overweight men, both of whom drank rather more than would be recommended. Both had similar life-styles, similar background and similar family histories; the only obvious difference was that one smoked heavily and the other never touched a cigarette. The non-smoker is still alive and looks as if, against the odds, he will 'make old bones'. Although the smoker was not my patient, I had the unenviable duty of telling his wife that her husband had died suddenly from a coronary.

Nearly half of all sudden cardiac-related deaths occur in heavy drinkers, and in these cases smoking is an additional risk factor. These sudden deaths are particularly likely to happen if the drinker has been bingeing. It is worrying that they can strike people who have reasonably clean coronary arteries. The deaths are attributed to a variety of causes: some are the result of a lethal arrhythmia (an irregular heartbeat which is incompatible with an effective pumping action of the heart), spasm in the coronary

arteries, sudden changes in the blood pressure which may dis-
lodge or rupture a coronary atheromatous plaque, or the consequences of an alcoholic cardiomyopathy. What should be
reassuring is that there is no increased incidence in any of these
conditions in those whose drinking is light or moderate; it is the
heavy binge drinkers who may suddenly crumple.

The findings of large-scale population studies have been supported by animal experiments. Rabbits have arteries which
respond even less well to a high-fat diet than does the human
cardiovascular system. In laboratories all over the world there
are rows of rabbit hutches in which the luckless incumbents are
being fed high-fat (or low-fat) diets, and after death the damage
to their arteries is compared.

One animal experiment of this nature took place at the Wister
Institute of Anatomy and Biology in Philadelphia. Two scientists,
David Clerfield and David Kritchevsky, compared the effect of
wine, beer and spirits on rabbits who had been enjoying glutto-
nous meals enriched with fats. The rabbits were allowed to drink
with their meals: some, the unluckiest ones, had water, the others
either had pure ethanol from the laboratory, spirits from the off-
licence, beer or wine. After a few months of this sybaritic life-
style, the coronary arteries of the rabbits were examined. Those
who had only water to drink with their meals had the worst
arteries; every one showed signs of coronary arterial disease.
Beer drinkers fared little better. The hearts of 86 per cent of those
drinking whisky and 75 per cent of those on pure ethanol were
affected by early signs of disease. The wine drinkers, conversely,
had to some extent been protected from the high fat diet: 67 per
cent of those on white wines had the fatty streaks in the arteries
that showed early degenerative changes, but only 40 per cent of
the rabbits whose food had been accompanied by red wine
demonstrated arterial disease.

Some recent research, on humans rather than rabbits, has
shown that some forms of beer drinking provide better protection than others. The dark brown beers really are, as the old
advertisements always suggested, 'good for you'. We now know

that dark beers contain more of the known flavonoids than light beer.

Since the 1970s debate has raged around the relative value of

"WHAT ABOUT LAGER IN A BROWN GLASS?"

different drinks to the long-term health of the drinker. Is the jolly farmer knocking back his beer in the George and Dragon less likely to have a coronary thrombosis than the aesthetic judge drinking his claret in the Reform Club or the plethoric colonel emptying the whisky bottle in the Cavalry Club? The evidence is that all will derive benefit, but that this will be greatest for the wine drinker. However, the choice of drink is only one of many factors in a person's life-style which determines longevity and resistance to coronary heart disease.

The opinion of Doctor St Leger, widely accepted for many years, was that wine probably contained a constituent that was cardio-protective, and that it was this substance, rather than the alcohol itself, which reduced the incidence of heart disease. This view has now been modified in the light of subsequent experiments, and the idea that it is wine, and only wine, which is beneficial does not entirely explain the evidence.

Initially, research suggesting that alcohol was cardio-protective tended to be discounted. Doctors suggested that the benefit from the wine was illusory: the apparent advantages were because wine drinkers tended to be rich and cosseted. Wine was in fact no more than an indication of the financial status of the drinker, and there was already a proven link between longevity and standard of living. This view totally failed to take into account the French Paradox, whereby peasants who drink wine survive to a remarkable age. Furthermore, later research carried out in population studies all around the world has investigated people of very varying life-styles and incomes: the light to moderate drinkers, particularly of red wine, invariably fare better, regardless of their background, than either the abstainers or those who drink to excess.

In 1995 the *British Medical Journal* reported on a survey carried out in Copenhagen. The research workers had followed 13,000 men and women to record their life-styles, including tobacco and alcohol intake and the effect on the subject's health. The findings showed that wine drinkers were indeed favoured by the gods, and enjoyed better health than those who were either abstainers or beer drinkers. Spirit drinkers in Copenhagen did only marginally better than teetotallers. If someone drank spirits occasionally, perhaps two to three times a month, there was some advantage; if they drank them regularly, they fared no worse than teetotallers, provided they had no more than two drinks a day; but if they had more, they were perhaps at a disadvantage. The wine drinkers had a death rate from heart disease which had apparently been cut by 60 per cent. Beer drinkers were not quite so well rewarded for their time at the bar: their death rate from coronary arterial disease was only cut by 30 per cent – but at least they did better than the abstainers.

An interesting feature of the Danish research, as with the study of American nurses, was that even drinking a fraction more than the two to four glasses of wine a day seemed to be beneficial, which rather undermines the British Ministry of Health's advice on safe limits.

Although the news about the heart for light to moderate drinkers, whether male or female, is good, for a few persistently heavy drinkers there may be a little-known but very serious cardiac problem. Mention the word 'Bollinger' at the bar, and an anticipatory smile will spread across the faces of the regulars. To those who enjoy a drink, the name is synonymous with good-quality champagne and conjures up memories of a hundred happy occasions. To a doctor who enjoys the occasional glass, however, the name also provokes some anxiety, because it was a certain Professor Bollinger who in 1884 first described alcoholic cardiomyopathy.

The doctor and his drinking companions can enjoy their Bollinger, happy in the knowledge that although red wines are better for the heart and circulation, in every way white wine is better than nothing – and most people are prepared to sacrifice some efficacy in order to enjoy champagne.

However, there is a cloud in the cardiovascular sky: cardiomyopathy. It is well known that too many drinks taken for too long may adversely affect the liver and in a small minority of cases lead to cirrhosis. It is less well known that an even smaller proportion of heavy drinkers may find that their habit has poisoned their heart muscle. Cardiomyopathy means no more than 'disease of the heart muscle'; it is now believed to be caused by the toxic effects of persistently high blood alcohol, and not, as used to be thought, by malnourishment and a deficiency of the vitamin thiamine, which can be a problem in heavy drinkers. Even the best-fed drinkers, whose champagne is followed by the healthiest of meals stacked with vegetables, wholemeal bread, fish and other nourishing foods, may still develop a cardiomyopathy.

Not every cardiomyopathy is related to alcohol. There are three types: hypertrophic, in which the heart muscle is grossly enlarged; restrictive, when the heart has been damaged by scarring or infiltration with non-muscular tissue; and finally, a dilated cardiomyopathy, which afflicts those who drink to excess. In cardiomyopathies, the heart outline is enlarged on X-ray, and very often tests show that it is inefficient and its rhythm is irregular.

Alcoholic cardiomyopathy affects men more often than women. This is the result of different drinking patterns, for in the development of cardiomyopathy, as in so many other aspects of heavy drinking, women have once again drawn the short straw. Just as women are more likely to get cirrhosis of the liver – and if they get it, the condition is less likely to respond to abstinence – so are they more likely to develop a cardiomyopathy. Women, partly because they are generally smaller and have a different proportion of body fat, require an alcohol intake only 60 per cent that of a man to run the same risk of developing the condition. However, as with cirrhosis, the drinking has to be not only heavy but prolonged. It is rare to diagnose alcoholic cardiomyopathy in a patient who has not been drinking heavily for at least ten to fifteen years. The damage to the heart muscle seems to be related to the cumulative dose of alcohol over the years; it can be technically described as a 'dose-dependent disease'.

Fortunately, most drinkers do not suffer from a cardiomyopathy, and it is still uncommon enough not to have become the basis of a barside horror story. When a patient is afflicted by alcohol cardiomyopathy the other body muscles, in particular those of the limbs, suffer similar changes. A biopsy of the muscles of the top of the arm will, for instance, often mirror the microscopic changes in muscle fibres that can be found in the heart.

The signs and symptoms of alcoholic cardiomyopathies have one rather sinister characteristic in common. Although a cardiomyopathy's presence may be detected by chest X-rays, ECGs and echocardiograms, it does not cause much trouble until it is well established, and then it strikes very quickly. Once patients start to develop breathlessness, swelling of the feet and the irregular heartbeat, they often go downhill rapidly. If they already have any other kind of heart disease, which is not unusual in middle-aged patients, the combination of that with cardiomyopathy can be particularly disabling.

A few years ago I was seconded to a hospital to stand in for a contemporary who had developed angina. Cardiologists found that his coronary artery disease was not particularly severe, but that its effects had been exaggerated by an alcoholic cardiomyopathy. The doctor never returned to work, but used to come round to the clinic for a chat from time to time. The interval between the chats became longer and longer, and the doctor died of heart failure within a year or so of the diagnosis of cardiomyopathy. In other cases, the irregular rhythm of the heart frequently found in patients with this condition may lead to strokes.

As with the overwhelming majority of diseases associated with drinking, alcoholic cardiomyopathy does not attack the light or moderate drinker. Like cirrhosis of the liver, it is a risk run only by heavy, regular drinkers. Fortunately, only a minority of heavy drinkers have to pay such a high price for having maintained their excessive intake for decades.

Demonstrable alcoholic cardiomyopathy is in fact a comparatively rare cause of irregular heartbeat in those who drink to excess. On the other hand, atrial fibrillation is frequently found amongst heavy drinkers. In this condition the heartbeat is irregularly irregular, which creates the basic problem: when the heart is fibrillating, the collecting chambers of the heart, the atria, beat so rapidly that in many cases the rate is too quick for the rhythm to be transmitted to the powerful pumping chambers, the ventricles, and the sequence of the heartbeat, with each of the chambers beating in time, is lost.

A heart which is irregular in this way becomes as inefficient as a car in which the valve timing has slipped, for if the human heart is to work efficiently its chambers need to beat in sequence. A patient who is fibrillating will notice sudden breathlessness; they may develop angina and suffer palpitations. The irregular action may also propel blood clots into the circulation, where if they obstruct an important artery, such as the one leading to the brain, the results can be disastrous. Very often the normal rhythm returns spontaneously, and if not, it can be restored by applying an electric shock with a defibrillator. If atrial fibrillation persists, carefully monitored anti-coagulation dramatically reduces the incidence of subsequent strokes. Heavy drinking is, however, only one of many causes of atrial fibrillation.

The famous eighteenth-century physician Dr Heberden noticed in 1772 that a 'nightcap' prevented nocturnal angina, but it was two hundred years before the effect of alcohol on this condition was scientifically investigated. In 1956 the *Journal of the American Medical Association* carried an account by Dr Russek of experiments in which a couple of double whiskies were compared with nitroglycerine as preventers of angina.

The mechanism by which alcohol relieves angina is complex. Dr Russek was surprised to find that, although whisky from the barman was just as good as glyceryl trinitrate at banishing the pain, it had no effect on the ECG. Conversely, the chemist's pills, unlike the drink, restored both the ECG tracing to normal and relieved the chest pain. Dr Russek postulated that the effect of the whisky was not so much that it dilated the coronary arteries, but that after a drink the way in which the brain interpreted chest pain changed.

The vasodilatory action of alcohol on peripheral blood vessels is well known, and it had seemed reasonable before Dr Russek's work to assume that this also happened to the coronary arteries. Later experiments showed that normal coronary arteries flowing through undamaged heart muscles are indeed dilated by alcohol, but that once a heart has been damaged by coronary heart disease it behaves differently.

After small quantities of alcohol, such as is provided by a double whisky, the patient frequently notices that the angina has disappeared. This relief from pain is because the coronary arteries have in fact dilated. However, when higher concentrations of alcohol flow through the coronary blood vessels, the dilated vessels contain so much blood that the damaged heart muscle is deprived of an adequate supply of oxygen and other nutrients. Once ischaemic – short of the essential oxygen – the damaged heart muscle protests in its customary way by becoming very painful. This phenomenon of one part of the body taking more than its allotted supply of blood is known as 'stealing'; in this case, the dilated coronary arteries are stealing the blood from the deprived heart muscle.

Another example of stealing can arise after a heavy meal, particularly if it is accompanied by heavy drinking. After too large a meal, the amount of blood directed to the digestive tract may bring on the typical post-prandial angina. Patients will complain that after they have enjoyed food and a few drinks, they are unable to walk as far without chest pain as they were before they had their dinner.

One of my patients who developed coronary heart disease in his forties was chairman of an international company, a role which necessitated constant air travel from one capital city to another. Each time my patient flew, he suffered angina. We tried all the standard anti-anginal agents without success, until one day, just before I had lunch with him, he handed me a powerful whisky. The whisky jogged my memory of Heberden's comments about alcohol in the early nineteenth century, and of Russek's research in the 1950s (when I was a medical student). I suggested that in future my patient should always have, regardless of the time of day, a strong whisky before he flew. Twenty-five years later the patient is still active, still travels the world, but tells me that he always has his whisky in the departure lounge. He has had many attacks of angina since our lunch together, but never when flying.

The way in which alcohol dilates the peripheral blood vessels can also have its dangers. Victorian paintings show St Bernards or bloodhounds with brandy barrels around their necks, accompanied by warmly clad monks, pawing the ashen face of a traveller buried in the snow. The traveller's feeble hands stretch out for the 'life-saving' brandy. This image has helped to perpetuate the myth that alcohol keeps out the cold and protects the life of the frozen traveller. Nothing could be further from the truth. Alcohol makes the drinker more liable to hypothermia, as the increased flow of blood through the skin exposes a greater proportion of the volume of blood to the chill of the winter night. The brandy undermines the body's own defence mechanism against the cold; without a stiff drink, the peripheral blood vessels would have constricted automatically once the person became chilled, and thereafter the blood would have been redirected to the deeper tissues where it would be kept warm by an insulating layer of subcutaneous fat.

The protection that alcohol taken in sensible quantities affords to the heart and blood vessels has been assumed to be bound up with the effect it has on blood fat levels. Previous research had encouraged the belief that half the cardio-protective effect of alcohol could be attributed to its ability to increase the HDL/total cholesterol ratio; only 18 per cent was attributed to its power to reduce the overall amount of low-density lipoprotein (LDL) levels.

Recent research suggests that it is the overall quantity of LDL which may be the dominant factor. LDL is the pernicious element in the overall cholesterol level: the fat which is deposited in the walls of the coronary arteries and which oozes out to form atheromatous plaques on the inside of the artery. In time, the arteries become narrowed so that the blood flow is impeded and the patient develops angina. From time to time one of the atheromatous plaques may rupture, which can lead to the formation of a thrombus (clot) that could block the arteries altogether. Both alcohol and the naturally occurring flavonoids influence the production of platelets – the particles in the blood involved in its clotting mechanism – by reducing their tendency to clump. Too much alcohol may affect the bone marrow's ability to produce platelets; too low a platelet count could cause a potentially dangerous tendency to bruise or bleed. This can be particularly important in heavy drinkers, who may be suffering from gastritis, gastric ulcers or enlarged veins in the oesophagus. Other factors involved in clotting are also affected by alcohol consumption: a moderate intake reduces the level of fibrinogen in the blood and therefore makes ischaemic strokes or thromboses in the coronary arteries less likely.

Not only does alcohol have an influence on the heart muscles and the arteries, but it also affects the constitution of the blood that flows through them. Blood cells are produced in the bone marrow, which is sensitive to alcohol. Liver damage can adversely affect the blood count. The white cells in the blood are part of the patient's immune system, the defence mechanism against infections. Damage to the white cell production, as well as a possibly adverse effect of alcohol on the lymphatic system, accounts for a heavy drinker's liability to succumb to secondary infections after an otherwise unimportant cough and cold, or minor surgery.

Research is continuing into ways in which alcohol may benefit the heart. It seems probable that flavonoids not only have a bearing on cholesterol levels, but may also have a protective influence on the structure of the arterial wall, and through this protection, help to keep the lining of the vessels free from plaques of atheroma. In addition to their antioxidant effect, there is evidence that the flavonoids in red wine relax the walls of the coronary arteries, thereby facilitating circulation of the blood.

Other antioxidants interact with the flavonoids and are therefore important in this process. At present these antioxidants are thought to include folic acid, beta-carotene, other carotenoids, and vitamin E.

Few branches of medicine have progressed so much in the last fifty years as the study of cardiology. There have been great advances in cardiac surgery, and many sufferers from heart disease owe their lives to this high-tech medicine. However, two simple substances, alcohol and aspirin, which have been available for centuries, have been found to have contributed to these advances.

4

Alcohol and hypertension

No visit to the doctor is complete without having one's blood pressure taken, yet an understanding of its significance is fairly rare amongst the general public. The doctor smiles knowingly and says, 'Ah, that's good – 130 over 80.' The patient is grateful for the reassurance, but usually has not the slightest idea what these magic figures mean.

High blood pressure, or hypertension, is of great importance when examining the consequences of drinking on health. There have been more than sixty major epidemiological studies and countless smaller surveys and trials assessing the effect of alcohol on blood pressure.

Blood pressure is the pressure transmitted from the heart to the arteries: the upper figure is the pressure when the main chambers of the heart are contracting, the lower figure when they are relaxed. If there was no pressure in the blood vessels during cardiac relaxation, the patient would faint seventy times a minute. To avoid this, the arterial walls are designed to maintain a sufficiently high pressure to keep the circulation moving and the brain and other vital organs supplied with oxygen and nutrients. The actual figure 130 is the height, measured in millimetres, of a column of mercury in the thin glass tube. The upper figure is referred to as the systolic pressure, the lower as the diastolic.

In Britain we are rather liberal with the limits we set, but certainly any reading which showed the systolic pressure as over 160 would be considered an indication of hypertension. Similarly, a diastolic of over 100 would warrant treatment. In practice, more and more doctors consider these limits too high, but in older patients bringing the diastolic down too low may be counter-productive.

There is no doubt that even moderate drinking – say three or four drinks a day – increases the blood pressure, but statistics show that this does not nullify the advantages of drinking. As we have seen, the death rate from cardiovascular diseases and all-cause mortality is lower in moderate drinkers.

One myth that needs to be exposed is that hypertension is a measure of a person's irri- tability. Any association bet- ween a high blood pressure and bad temper is indirect. Many patients are still rather offended when first told they have hypertension. The reac- tion of one was, 'Don't be so bloody rude,' which sums up the lay view that a high blood pressure is synonymous with a choleric temper.

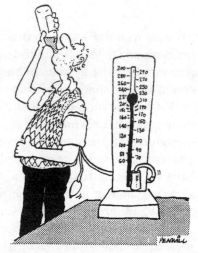

Some bad-tempered people who are tense and edgy may indeed have hypertension, as tem- perament does have an effect on the blood pressure, but it is not an invariable rule. Some very irritable old men have a low blood pressure, while some with an angelic temperament are hyperten- sive.

Persistent low blood pressure is not considered abnormal in Britain, and therefore does not require treatment. On the Continent, however, this condition is sometimes treated. Even if British doctors do not treat low blood pressure, they do recog- nize that patients with a persistently low reading are often aes- thetic and sensitive, and regard their propensity to suffer from lack of energy and depression as a feature of their temperament rather than symptoms of an illness. Conversely, European doc- tors regard these patients' psychological make-up as a response to the low blood pressure.

The two best-known American population studies enquiring

into life-style, and therefore drinking habits and health in general, are the review of the 87,526 American nurses mentioned already (see p. 49) and the Framingham Study. In the latter, the community of Framingham was chosen as being representative of an American town. The inhabitants' way of life was closely evaluated, and the effect of variations within it on the incidence of cardiovascular and other diseases was analysed. Both surveys, which were subject to meticulous statistic control, showed an increase in the incidence of hypertension in drinkers, and the Framingham Study demonstrated that high blood pressure is twice as common in heavy than light drinkers.

The effect of alcohol on blood pressure is independent of its tendency to make the drinker gain weight. Although some of the increase in blood pressure in heavy drinkers may be related to their increased bulk, even if they remain as thin as a model there is every chance that their blood pressure will rise.

Medical views differ as to the mechanism and significance of the hypertension found in drinkers. In 1995 the prestigious scientific journal *Clinical Experimental Pharmacology and Physiology* published in the same issue, and next door to each other, two reviews of the association between alcohol and hypertension. Both groups of authors were united in their belief that there was overwhelming evidence of a link. However conclusive the evidence that drinking even modest amounts increased the blood pressure, the experts differed as to the clinical importance of this rise.

The effect of alcohol on blood pressure is greater in older than in younger people. As people grow old, more and more life-style factors and bodily changes interact to cause an increase in blood pressure, of which alcohol may be just one. Although alcohol does have a specific effect on blood pressure, even in moderate drinkers, many personality traits and professional tensions contribute to the desire to drink, and many of these factors may also have a deleterious effect on blood pressure.

Those doctors who would minimize the effect of alcohol-induced hypertension on a patient's general health draw attention to the way in which blood pressure which has risen in response to alcohol rapidly falls to normal within a matter of weeks if a person subsequently becomes abstemious.

These doctors also emphasize that modest drinking offers protection against coronary heart disease and ischaemic strokes at the same time as it is causing a rise in blood pressure, whereas in most cases the higher the blood pressure, the greater the incidence of all strokes. The risk of a haemorrhagic stroke – one caused by bleeding from a cerebral blood vessel – is, however, greater in heavy drinkers with severe hypertension, and as the alcohol also acts as an anti-coagulant, the ability of the blood to clot is reduced.

Some specialists have even suggested that alcohol does not cause true persistent hypertension, merely a transient rise in blood pressure. Even so, these optimists recommend that patients with hypertension should cut their alcohol intake.

Light to moderate drinkers are less likely to have an ischaemic stroke – one brought on by an aberrant clot blocking a cerebral artery. This beneficial effect does not apply to those whose are binge drinkers.

Many of the regulars at the George and Dragon will swear that their blood pressure, and with it their propensity to strokes, is reduced because they are careful not to mix grain and grape. Others say with tremendous authority, as they down their eighth pint, 'Don't worry, doctor, I'm all right, I never drink spirits.' The truth is that the precautions taken to reduce the likelihood of ischaemic strokes should be the same as those adopted to reduce the risk of a coronary thrombosis.

To help prevent either a stroke or a heart attack, alcohol can be drunk in moderation, and in this respect red wine is particularly helpful. Heavy drinking is harmful, and heavy drinkers are more likely to suffer ischaemic strokes than are teetotallers or light to moderate drinkers.

As we have seen, the other type of stroke commonly diagnosed is the haemorrhagic, where part of the brain is destroyed by bleeding from a blood vessel which has ruptured or leaked. Blood vessels weakened by age or disease are more likely to give way if the blood pressure is raised. There is no doubt that keeping the blood pressure to normal levels will dramatically reduce the risk of suffering a haemorrhagic stroke: persuading heavy drinkers to become more modest consumers is part of the standard treatment for hypertensive patients.

Some years ago a survey was carried out of the day and time when patients who had suffered a haemorrhagic stroke were admitted to hospital. There was a clear relationship between these strokes and a heavy drinking session. In some cases, the stories are rather sad: the man who normally drinks very sensibly is led astray at a club dinner, only to regain consciousness – if he is lucky – in the local neurological ward.

One such case was that of a dynamic, early middle-aged entrepreneur who gave a lavish dinner party to celebrate a successful deal, where as usual he was a generous host and the best wines flowed freely. By the following morning he had suffered a massive stroke. This case also illustrates a curious feature of the rise in blood pressure that occurs after drinking: the pressure may go down for several hours before it rises.

Ischaemic strokes are also more common after binge drinking, unless the binge was with red wine. In instances where binge drinking has induced an ischaemic stroke, it is probably because the drinking has caused a cardiac arrhythmia. When I was a casualty doctor, Friday and Saturday nights were always hectic, not least because of the number of patients who came in through the receiving room having overdone the weekend drinking and suffered the dire consequences.

Studying the relationship between strokes and drinking underlines the message that the advantages of alcohol are derived from drinking regularly and not to excess. It is said that in some Mediterranean countries where regular drinking is the social pattern, the excessive drinker is in greater danger of suffering cirrhosis or cardiomyopathy. By contrast, in the cooler northern countries, where the drinking public are abstemious for five days and heavy drinkers for two, there is an increased incidence of sudden death from strokes and cardiac arrhythmias.

5

Alcohol and reproduction

Bacchus was the god of wine, but in ancient Rome his power was thought to lie in the realms of fertility and potency; the ability of wine to influence the physical condition of the heart would not be known for another two thousand years. But although the worship of Bacchus, with all its merrymaking, may have kept the blood flowing through the coronary arteries of the citizens of Rome, it is unlikely to have done much for either their potency or even their fertility. The Bacchanalian festivities were noted for their excesses, and probably only the virility of the youngest of the legionaries could have withstood the amount of wine drunk.

Bacchus's important responsibilities stemmed from the fact that the vine and wine had become identified with regeneration, and thus had a symbolic role in the furtherance of fertility. The dramatic rebirth of spring in a countryside covered in vines, when the dull brown hues of winter are replaced by a verdant foliage, exemplifies the indestructibility of life. Each year the seemingly near-dead vine bursts into vibrant life and provides a bountiful harvest. Noah's first action on stepping out of the ark on to dry land was to plant a vine.

Bacchus, the son of Zeus, had a liberal education: he was taught by satyrs, nymphs and centaurs together with Pan, the god of the woods and pastures. Priapus, another of his teachers, looked after agriculture. As the god of garden and field, Priapus had within his remit command of the vineyards. It would be a foolishly brave Roman who failed to acknowledge the virtues of the vine and its wine, because they had been taught that to do so would subject them to the dreadful fate of Pentheus. He had rejected Bacchus and all that he stood for, and suffered the penalty of being torn to pieces by the frenzied female members of his own family. This was an early indication that Bacchanalian parties can be dangerous if carried to extremes.

Priapus also became a symbol for manhood. Every sixth-former who has studied classical civilization has gazed in awe and sometimes envy at pictures of the famous statue of the god with his enormous erect penis. There is some irony in this, for just as the influence of wine on the cardiovascular system is good, it does not require a knowledge of Shakespeare to know that its effect on potency in particular, and reproduction in general, is discouraging. If Priapus had practised what he preached when he taught Bacchus about wine, he would not have been the proud god portrayed in the literature.

Too much alcohol does nothing for male potency. Temporary impotence after a heavy night's drinking is said to be the result of stupor; this explanation is almost certainly too simplistic. It is more likely that the wine has an anaesthetizing effect on the peripheral cutaneous nerves leading to the penis and the nerve supply to its blood vessels.

The anaesthetic effect of brandy, which was so useful to the nineteenth-century surgeon when the patient was on the table, can equally well dull the senses of the lover before he, or she, climbs into bed. Transitory impotence after heavy drinking, the 'brewer's droop' so often described in magazines, is always thought to be a male problem, but in fact the equivalent female response is also dulled. The woman who has drunk to excess – and in some cases this may only be three or four glasses of wine – may not only lose her ability to have an orgasm but also, although emotionally enthusiastic, may lose her physical response. Her lack of arousal may draw the evening to an early conclusion.

The effect of even small quantities of wine on female sexual response was explored by a colleague of mine when he came as an assistant to my practice in Norfolk. He and his partner stayed with us for some months and we dined together each night. For a time I could not understand why my colleague's usually

"I'M SORRY - I FORGOT TO STOP AT TWO GLASSES"

healthy appetite for wine was now so strictly controlled. After a couple of glasses all round, he would ostentatiously announce that he thought that we had had enough. It was a week or two before he confessed the truth: it took two glasses of wine to relax his girlfriend to the point where she wanted sex – but any more and she was incapable of enjoying it.

The long-term effects of drinking on the reproductive system are even more significant. Alcohol taken in excess for a number of years produces marked physical changes in both sexes. In men there is testicular atrophy, shrinkage of the penis, a loss of body hair and gynaecomastia or enlargement of the breasts. The body shape changes too: there is an acceleration of the normal redistribution of fat and loss of muscle that occurs in both sexes as they grow older. The arms and legs become skinny and the chest and abdomen increase in girth. Men develop the drinker's pot belly. Research has shown that there is a direct relationship between the possession of a 'beer belly' and the likelihood of being impotent. Recent studies in Russia have suggested that one in three early middle-aged Russian males are impotent as the result of persistent heavy drinking. Russia has the highest consumption of alcohol per capita in the world, but without studying the survey in detail it would be difficult to know what credence to give these statistics.

The popular explanation for the long-term changes that occur in the male reproductive system is that the oestrogen/testosterone balance is upset as the result of hormonal changes secondary to liver disease. Oestrogens are the hormones which determine femininity; testosterone is the hormone which gives the male his distinctive physique and personality. It is supposed that the damaged liver fails to metabolize adequately the oestrogens which circulate in all men. In addition, the testosterone is metabolized differently and rapidly to oestradiol.

The combination of these two processes decreases the amount of testosterone and increases the oestrogen. As if this were not damaging enough to a man's self-image, there is yet another obstacle to his ambition to look like a youthful Atlas. Not all testosterone is free testosterone, that is, readily available in a form which can be utilized by the tissues. In men with liver disease, much of the testosterone is not free, and is therefore comparatively useless at imparting male characteristics.

A quick glance around the dinner table will usually reveal that many men have 'liver palms', one of the signs of liver disease. The fleshy portions of the palm are bright red but the back of the hands remain pale, so that there is a 'Plimsoll line' between the back of the hand and the palm. This condition is not only seen in heavy drinkers but also in women when they

THE FINE FIGURE OF A HEAVY SOCIAL DRINKER

are pregnant or taking the pill, two states in which there are high levels of oestrogen circulating.

The effects of heavy drinking on men are not all related to liver damage: high blood levels of alcohol also have a directly damaging influence on testicular function. The Leydig cells in the testes, which secrete testosterone, are vulnerable to alcohol. In heavy drinkers, therefore, not only has the metabolism of testosterone and oestrogen been altered but also the actual secretion of testosterone reduced.

The changes in a man are not confined to his anatomy and physiology; his psyche is also altered. The heavy drinker progressively loses his libido as his testosterone levels fall. It is surprising how often heavy drinkers tell me that the women of today do not compare with those of their youth: they are neither as sexually attractive nor as witty. Dinner parties would be a bore, the heavy drinker says, if it were not for the wine. Men with a low testosterone level do not realize that female company is just the same as it has always been, and that the only difference lies with their own personality, which has changed as their desires have ebbed away because of a falling hormone level.

Fathering a child in old age is usually worth a paragraph or two in the local paper. It is unlikely that many of these septuagenarian dads will have been heavy drinkers, as high blood alcohol levels not only damage the Leydig cells in the testes but also the semeniferous tubes where the sperm are formed, thus impairing spermatogenesis. Research published in the journal *Gastroenterology* in 1974 showed that 80 per cent of alcoholics were infertile. Consistently heavy drinking affects the sperm count, and more of the sperm are of abnormal form. Sperm motility is also reduced: they are less likely to swim strongly and in the right direction. To achieve maximum fertility, sperm have to swim with the determination of a greyhound springing from the traps.

Although less obvious, the effects of excessive alcohol are equally trying in women. The bodily changes they experience

echo those found in men. There is some shrivelling of the external genitalia and a loss of pubic and other bodily hair. The
drinker tends to develop a pot belly, large breasts and skinny
arms and legs. The higher circulating level of oestrogen, whilst
it may have other advantages, is responsible for the heavier
breasts. However, women who drink in moderation need not
fear that their female physical characteristics will disappear
prematurely.

As always, the problem here is that warnings about drinking
to excess are also directed at women who drink at reasonable levels. This is demonstrated by the general approach to osteoporosis. No family health guide or women's magazine fails to
mention the fact that alcohol contributes to osteoporosis, but few
add that, whereas alcoholism and alcohol abuse are accepted risk
factors, there fortunately seems to be little association between
bone density and light to moderate alcohol intake. Various
research studies have shown that bone density in post-
menopausal women is not affected by modest drinking. As these
studies have examined women who drink five to fourteen units
a week and found no significant increase in the incidence of hip
fracture, it seems safe to tell women that a daily drink – or perhaps even two – will not make their bones brittle.

As for women who drink during their reproductive years, the
main concern has been for the babies they might conceive. The
level of anxiety in the USA and Canada about drinking during
pregnancy seems to the British to be out of all proportion to the
dangers.

No one denies the existence or seriousness of Foetal Alcohol
Syndrome (FAS), a group of malformations which give the child
born to a heavy-drinking, and usually socially deprived, mother
a very characteristic appearance, but this is said by the *Oxford
Textbook of Medicine*, the average doctor's authoritative guide to
the practice of medicine, to occur only in women who regularly
drink more than 2 to 2.5 ounces (at least four units) of alcohol
daily throughout early pregnancy. Furthermore, population
studies have shown that there is a greater risk of suffering FAS

if the mother lives in an inner city. Although the overwhelming majority of inner-city dwellers are well nourished and do credit to the care provided by a welfare state, the incidence of malnourishment in these areas is higher than in the population at large.

In 1987 a study carried out in America of 32,870 women, nearly half of whom had taken alcohol during pregnancy, failed to find one case of Foetal Alcohol Syndrome. Another survey showed that FAS had a direct relationship to prosperity; it was almost absent in the presumably better-nourished sections of society.

In Foetal Alcohol Syndrome, the child affected is small: weight, length and skull circumference at birth are all reduced. The eyes are smaller than average, with an apparent squint, and the bridge of the nose is poorly developed, giving a snub-nosed look. The chin is also poorly developed, and the ears are big, flat and badly modelled, with a lack of contours. The face suffers from varying degrees of absence of the skin folds around the upper lip. The general effect is of a mentally retarded, small-headed pixie.

The problems of a child with FAS are not confined to external appearance: they are also liable to suffer from congenital heart disease and abnormalities of the joints. Not all of the signs are present in affected children, and no single sign can be considered essential to the diagnosis. One patient of mine, who was prosperous and middle-class but an exceptionally heavy drinker, had a child with a slightly small head and abnormal ears but no other signs of FAS; fortunately, the child was not retarded.

Discussion of Foetal Alcohol Syndrome is always confused by the lesser problems which, though not associated with any obvious physical signs of the syndrome, do seem to affect children of heavy drinkers. These ill-defined symptoms are lumped together as the Foetal Alcohol Effect Syndrome (FAEs). Children of very heavy-drinking mothers tend to be smaller than their peers; they suck less well after delivery and do not put on weight so readily. They are more excitable and easily disturbed than other babies.

Features of the Foetal Alcohol Syndrome

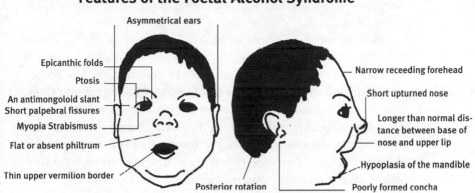

The neo-prohibitionists claim that even by the time the children of drinking mothers reach primary school, they do less well in class with regard to both academic performance and social integration. Doubts have recently been expressed about whether FAEs is a distinct entity, and if it is, how much is due to alcohol and how much to maternal deprivation.

Research has shown that there is little reduction in birth weight and size if women drink less than ten to twelve units a week – unless they also smoke. Mothers who both smoke and drink immediately before and during pregnancy run the risk of having children of lower birth weight. The *American Journal Of Public Health* says the available data suggests that women's smoking habits should be taken into consideration when advice is given about drinking.

Binge drinking in pregnancy has also been investigated, and there is evidence that in some very rare cases as few as five units in a single sitting may have contributed to a low birth weight. However, in forty years of medicine I have looked after a large number of mothers who knew that their babies were conceived after an evening's heavy drinking, or who had drunk heavily before they were even aware they were pregnant, and the good news is that none of the children show evidence of the symptoms ascribed to FAEs. Surprisingly, a recent report (1995)

73

showed that the babies of women who were light drinkers in pregnancy had slightly heavier babies than those who did not drink at all.

I therefore feel confident in reassuring a mother who has been 'caught out' by her pregnancy, but even so, it is a wise precaution not to drink heavily if pregnancy is a possibility. The advice I give to women is that they need not be teetotal when pregnant, but that they should only drink at a formal or special occasion and with a meal, and they should not exceed two units in any one evening or seven units in the week. This is being cautious, but thankfully our knowledge of obstetrics has come a long way since Old Testament times, when Samson's mother was ordered:

Thou shalt conceive and bear a son, now drink no wine or strong drink.

If a previously heavy-drinking woman is being prescribed Antabuse to help her stay sober, it is very important that she should not become pregnant. Antabuse is a drug given to bolster the patient's determination not to drink; if they take alcohol after a dose of it, they not only feel very sick but also sweaty and desperately ill. In the first three months of pregnancy Antabuse is much more likely to cause foetal abnormalities than an excess of wine taken at a dinner party.

Nutrition is important for women who wish to become pregnant. It is known that blood folate levels are reduced by alcohol, and it is also known that taking folic acid dramatically cuts the number of children born with foetal abnormalities. All women intending to become pregnant should take additional folic acid in the dosage recommended by the Department of Health. Women who regularly enjoy a few glasses of wine each day and who hope to become pregnant should be particularly assiduous in taking this harmless dietary supplement, and would be well advised to discuss with their doctor whether to take the higher dose advised for women whose babies might be at particular risk. They should also cut their wine intake in anticipation.

Women who continue to drink heavily while pregnant are also very much more likely to miscarry during the first six months of the pregnancy.

The recognition of FAS has brought disadvantages as well as advantages to women. A great fear of the condition has been unnecessarily induced in many women; they live through forty weeks of anxiety, wondering whether that half a bottle of wine before they knew they had conceived will have damaged their baby. Women who continue to have the occasional drink when pregnant sometimes suffer prejudice from family, friends and workmates who are unaware of the true facts. Recently, a colleague was dining in New York when his hostess noticed that a pregnant guest was helping herself to a glass of wine. The hostess refused to let it pass, and said that she did not want to be party to the birth of a mentally retarded, physically deformed child. When my colleague suggested that there was no evidence from anywhere in the world, even the most deprived ghetto, to back such an extreme view, she became distressed, refused to continue with the dinner and the evening ended in chaos. People should be reminded that even the US authorities, while recommending no alcohol during pregnancy, admit there is general agreement that a single daily drink (one unit) will do no harm.

On a happier note, Jane MacQuitty, Jancis Robinson and Alice King, all of them well known wine writers, have continued to work full time and to drink in moderation throughout their combined ten pregnancies. Their children are all developing normally and appear as attractive and intelligent to the rest of the world as they do to their loving parents and grandparents.

Alcohol is excreted in breast milk, and breast-feeding women are recommended not to have more than the odd glass, although it is unlikely to do more than make the baby drowsy. According to a warning in the *Oxford Textbook of Medicine*, the children of breast-feeding alcoholic mothers have suffered from blood clotting and bleeding into vital organs. It is therefore not a good way to ensure that mother and child get a good night's sleep, although the Oxford textbook also reassures women that no adverse effects have ever been reported in the breast-fed children of social drinkers.

Empty your glass before you allow it to be refilled.

Avoid drinking at both lunchtime and in the evening.

Flavonoids are more abundant in red wine and dark beers than in other drinks. It is this abundance which gives these drinks an advantage, but other drinks also have a health-giving value.

Not all wines, even if the same colour, have equal cardioprotective qualities; flavonoid content depends on the type of grape, the nature of the soil, climate and the way in which the wine is made.

6

Alcohol and digestion

The use of alcohol as an aid to digestion is no new concept. In the Middle Ages Saint Benedict of Aniane, whose order ran the famous monastery of Cluny, insisted that the monastic meals be accompanied by at least one-third of a bottle of wine. Centuries later Erasmus – humanist, philosopher and good friend of Saint Thomas More – wrote that he relied on wine to shake up his digestion. Nearer to our own times, the eighteenth-century French philosopher Helvétius said:

> There is nothing wrong with wine taken in moderation, as it is useful and even necessary to facilitate the digestion and fortify the stomach.

The traditional glass of sherry before a meal sharpens the appetite, stimulates the gastric mucosa (lining) and relaxes both host and guest so that they are mentally and physically able to enjoy their meal. Saint Benedict of Aniane has blessed the custom of serving wine with food, but the tradition of the aperitif stretches even further back. The ancient Romans used wine to stimulate the appetite, and the habit of drinking before meals had become firmly established in Britain by the seventeenth century.

Although in the moderate drinker a glass of champagne or sherry encourages the appetite, research has shown that heavy drinkers almost invariably have a poor appetite and develop characteristic likes and dislikes in food. Watch a heavy drinker settle down at the restaurant table: he may well make a hog of himself with the butter and will wade into the roast beef with relish, but he will fight shy of vegetables and wholemeal bread. Heavy drinkers are also able to enjoy fatty and high-protein foods without making their indigestion worse.

Although alcohol stimulates the appetite, it does not, perhaps surprisingly, stimulate the production of saliva. If there is an increase in spit production during the pre-dinner drinks, it is not through any direct action of the alcohol on the salivary glands, but because the thought of the food and drink has encouraged the guests to salivate in anticipation.

When one is drinking, the parotid glands (the glands which swell with mumps) and the salivary glands produce less saliva; therefore the food tends to be more dry, which can contribute to difficulties in swallowing. The lack of saliva is one of the reasons – as well as the dehydration – why after a 'good dinner' it is common to wake up with a parched, dry throat, a tongue which sticks to the roof of the mouth and teeth that have to be scrubbed clean.

Heavy drinkers suffer from sialadenosis, swelling of the salivary glands, which is very obvious if the parotid glands are involved. It is these swollen parotids found in regular drinkers which cause 'chipmunk' or 'hamster' cheeks, a characteristic frequently used by cartoonists to lampoon elderly, red-faced colonels.

There are many other causes of chronic swelling of the parotids, and as with dysphagia, it should not be attributed to the daily dose of claret until all the potentially nastier reasons have been excluded. Even drinkers should take note of the enlarged parotid, as there is some evidence that it is more common in those who have liver damage.

The oesophagus is not immune to the effects of over-indulgence either; it can become chronically inflamed. This inflammation, known as oesophagitis, affects the lower end of the gullet, behind the sternum, producing the classic burning pain known as heartburn. Oesophagitis strikes in the early hours of the morning, and drives people from their beds to go in search of soothing milk or antacids.

Oesophagitis is sometimes associated with a reflux of stomach acid into the oesophagus, giving rise to the sensation of 'acid-brash'. Heavy drinkers, particularly if they have been on a binge, are prone to these symptoms. Experiments have been performed in which ethanol, beers, wines and spirits have been dripped straight into the stomach. It was found that, when in the form bought from the brewery or wine merchants, the alcohol produced more acidity and reflux than did the alcohol solution bought from the chemists.

Interestingly, although some oesophageal reflux can be demonstrated in the majority of people who have been drinking, most did not experience pain or discomfort, and on examination the reflux was only associated with oesophagitis in a minority of cases. This reflux of stomach acid into the gullet, together with the alcoholic fumes which may be given off from the stomach contents, can ruin an opera singer's voice, which is why they are advised not to drink for several days before they sing. Many people, particularly as they grow older, notice that their voices are husky after a night's drinking, and if they could view their own laryngeal cords on the diagnostic screen, they would be surprised to see how red and swollen they were.

It is thought that heartburn and chest pain can be caused by changes in oesophageal motility as well as by inflammation of the mucosa. Experiments have demonstrated that heavy drinkers show abnormalities in their motility. The effect of this on the oesophageal peristalsis can cause problems with swallowing, including the sensation that food is sticking on the way down. This symptom, known as dysphagia, can be the result of chronic scarring of the gullet, the presence of an unusual ring of enlarged muscle, or less frequently, malignant growths. Any difficulty in swallowing should be investigated immediately.

The stomach lining is able to adapt to a wide variety of irritants. Even so, some spirits are too strong to stimulate the production of gastrin – a hormone involved in the production of gastric acid, and hence in digestion – whereas more dilute alcoholic drinks, beer and wine, do encourage production. Too hefty a glass of whisky before dinner may cause gastric inflammation so severe in some people that it is possible to demonstrate a minimal ooze of blood from the gastric mucosa rather than any assistance with the flow of gastric juices.

Absorption of alcohol from the stomach depends on a great many factors, including the concentration and nature of the drink, whether it is being taken on a full or an empty stomach, and the individual characteristics of the drinker, including their gender. The advantage of drinking on a full stomach is that the alcohol then tends to be absorbed mainly through the stomach and does not pass into the duodenum so quickly; once in the duodenum, alcohol is absorbed into the bloodstream very rapidly. Recent evidence has also shown that after a good meal alcohol is not only absorbed more slowly but is metabolized faster. This accounts for the common observation that it is easier and quicker to get drunk at a cocktail party than while enjoying a good dinner.

One reason why alcohol is processed by the body less efficiently when the drinker is hungry is that fasting reduces the level of alcohol dehydrogenase (ADH), a naturally produced enzyme which metabolizes alcohol. In women the ADH system works rather better as they grow older, but the converse is true in men. Pre-menopausal women have a raw deal when drinking because their stomachs have only half as much ADH as men. Fortunately, most of the body's ADH is in fact supplied by the liver – in the male, 80 per cent of ADH is produced by the liver, 20 per cent by the stomach – but even so, this deficiency of the female stomach means that younger women achieve a higher blood alcohol level faster than men, even though they have drunk no more than their male companions, and tend to sober up less quickly. There are other factors which account for the female response to alcohol, but certainly the male chauvinist who believes that it is determined by a deficiency in the female personality, or even intellect, could not be more wrong.

Middle age does have some unexpected consolations for women: one jolly, roistering woman I have known since we were both teenagers used to be unable to have more than a drink or two in the evenings without feeling rather light-headed, but now she proudly says that she can drink any man under the table. It seems unkind to tell her that it is only because she is now post-menopausal: her ADH levels are higher and her hormonal balance is more masculine – more testosterone, less oestrogen. Presumably, HRT (hormone replacement therapy) will perpetuate the pre-menopausal female stomach's reaction.

Chronic gastritis, inflammation of the gastric mucosa, is common in heavy drinkers. Who has not heard the terrible sounds coming from the bathroom early in the morning when a very heavy drinker has come to stay? The hawking and retching is usually attributed by the sufferer to the smoking which so often accompanies heavy drinking, but we who watched him at the port the night before know the truth. The nausea tends to wear off by mid-morning, so he can enjoy his coffee-break and may even be able to take a bite of lunch. Breakfast, however, is out of the question.

Various surveys have shown that up to 70 per cent of people who regularly drink too much have inflammation of the gastric lining. Doctors have still not agreed on why this occurs, and it is difficult to reproduce experimentally. Some experts feel that the chronic gastritis of the heavy drinker is an indirect rather than direct effect of the alcohol: it has been suggested that malnutrition

" I FEEL THAT PREGNANCY IS NOT A VERY LIKELY CAUSE OF YOUR RECURRENT MORNING VOMITING, MR. BRAHMS "

and the reflux of intestinal contents back into the stomach is the cause of the chronic inflammation rather than the drink itself.

Research carried out at the University of Padova in Italy in 1992 showed a very clear association between the amount a patient smoked and the development of chronic atrophic gastritis in those who also drink. As in many other aspects of health, the combination of smoking and heavy drinking seems particularly liable to cause trouble. All too often the drink is blamed where it is only partly responsible; in truth, it is the synergy between the two habits that does the damage.

Not all the indigestion of heavy drinkers originates from the stomach. Alcohol affects the functions of the small intestine, influencing both its blood supply and its motility; little wonder that drinking worsens the symptoms of a duodenal ulcer.

Within the last few years it has become accepted that infection with the small organism *Helicobacter pylori* is responsible for peptic ulceration, whether the ulcer is in the stomach or the duodenum, and for some forms of gastro-intestinal inflammation. It had been hoped that alcohol might eradicate this organism. This has been shown to be true in older people, but unfortunately this is one of the advantages which only comes, along with the bus pass, at the age of sixty-five. In younger people, drinking tends to be associated with an increased incidence of *Helicobacter pylori* infection. Those of middle age fall between the two groups: alcohol seems to make little difference to them either way.

It is often believed that comparatively strong but bland drinks such as champagne delude the body so that the stomach empties quickly and the alcohol is rapidly absorbed from the small intestine. This is thought to account for the immediate response to champagne and hence its popularity on celebratory occasions. It requires only a couple of glasses for the decibel count to rise, whereas the hush of the club smoking room is not disturbed by the whisky-drinking members, whose pyloruses – the exit from their stomachs – have closed after the first few tension-relieving sips.

There is evidence that the strength of a drink determines how quickly it passes through the stomach and into the small intestine. Alcohol is not metabolized at all in the small bowel, either in men or women, but in both sexes it is absorbed more rapidly once it has reached the intestines than it is through the stomach wall. Although strong drinks are absorbed through the stomach wall, this may not be as important in determining the immediate blood alcohol levels as the speed at which the drink passes from the stomach to the small intestine. There is scientific evidence that spirits delay gastric emptying, and may therefore have a less rapid effect on sobriety, particularly if drunk on a full stomach, than some of the blander drinks.

Jeffrey Bernard's medical problems have filled many column inches of *The Spectator*, *Private Eye* and other journals. His initial trouble seemed to be chronic pancreatitis, which can later lead to pancreatic failure and diabetes. The pancreas is the major digestive organ of the body, as it is the manufacturing centre for the necessary enzymes. Within it are the Islets of Langerhans, or endocrine gland, which produce insulin. The average diabetic should be able to drink in moderation: they will adjust their treatment to take account of it as they would with any other food. However, heavy drinking can make the control of severe diabetes problematic.

Pancreatitis is usually a painful disease, though it can occasionally be relatively pain-free. Either way, once chronic pancreatitis develops, the condition tends to be progressive and the patient ends up with diabetes and poor digestion, characterized by steatorrhoea, a persistent diarrhoea with foul, fat-laden faeces. Jeffrey Bernard has not told us about his guts, but he has given us heart-rending accounts of his diabetes and the complications which have arisen from it. Three-quarters of all cases of pancreatitis are related to chronic alcoholism or disease of the biliary tract, and five per cent of heavy drinkers either have attacks of acute pancreatitis or develop the chronic form.

Jeffrey Bernard fits the description of the typical patient: he is male, middle-aged and, according to his autobiographical writing, no mean drinker. The outlook for a patient with acute pancreatitis is not good. Within ten years of the disease reaching the chronic stage, pancreatic insufficiency supervenes and in time proves fatal.

Although pancreatitis is more common in men, this is because more men than women drink to excess. Paradoxically, dose for dose, women are more likely to suffer pancreatic disease than men – yet another example of the need for them to remain light to moderate drinkers. An attack of acute pancreatitis is heralded by severe abdominal pain in the upper central area which radiates through to the back. The onset is very sudden, so much so that it can be confused with a perforated ulcer. The pain is difficult to relieve, even with the strongest narcotics, and the abdomen is very tender.

In all cases of acute abdominal pain, the possibility of pancreatitis always worries the doctor. Acute pancreatitis is not easy to diagnose, but various blood tests are helpful. If the attack is at all severe, the patient will usually need non-surgical treatment in an intensive care unit. In the past, it was always considered that surgery to treat pancreatitis was risky – the outcome often confirmed that it had been a grave error of judgement – but now, as intensive care has improved, surgery is undertaken more frequently.

Chronic pancreatitis is often the result of alcoholism, but whether this always follows minor attacks of acute pancreatitis that may have passed unnoticed is disputed. The patient suffers varying degrees of recurrent upper central abdominal (epigastric) pain, steatorrhoea and in time develops diabetes. All pancreatitis is associated with severe generalized weight loss due to malabsorption.

A heavy alcohol intake is associated not only with a diseased pancreas but also a rise in the blood level of triglycerides, one of the blood fats related to an increased risk of cardiovascular disease. Changes in the level of triglycerides may be one reason why the protective effect of moderate alcohol consumption is lost once the drinker indulges to excess.

Recent research on pancreatitis has suggested that the standard teaching on the disease may have to be modified. There is some good and some bad news for drinkers. It seems that the percentage of cases of pancreatitis which can be attributed to heavy drinking may have been overestimated. Research has shown that about one third of the cases of pancreatitis are related to excessive drinking, a third to gallstones and in the remaining third the underlying cause is undetected. It is possible that in this last group of patients there may be some who are drinking more than they admit, or their doctors estimate, but, if so, other tests have not revealed this. The bad news is that careful analysis of earlier surveys makes it possible that doctors have been too reassuring when handing on the previously received opinion that there is no association between cancer of the pancreas and chronic pancreatitis. There may indeed be a link, but it is not a very strong one.

There is a long-established theory that this same rise in triglycerides predisposes patients to pancreatitis, but doubts have recently been cast on its validity. Similarly, there have been attempts to link the type of drink taken with the propensity to pancreatitis. Well-researched papers have convincingly shown that the disease is more common in wine drinkers. Unfortunately, equally distinguished scientists are equally convincing in their arguments that pancreatitis is more common in beer or spirits drinkers. Since research has produced contradictory results, the present teaching is that the type of drink does not affect the likelihood of developing pancreatitis. It is now thought that the overall quantity of alcohol drunk is the relevant factor, and that the discrepancy between the research papers was the result of regional differences in drinking patterns that had influenced the selection of patients to be studied.

The function of the gall bladder, the reservoir for bile – which is essential to digestion – is improved by alcohol. Recent research using ultrasonography has shown that a dose of alcohol speeds the emptying of the gall bladder after a meal. It also accelerates the filling of the same bladder, and this increase in flow is thought to have a protective effect against gallstone formation. Wine is better than spirits or beer in protecting a drinker from this condition. Traditionally, the gallstone sufferer is said to be 'fair, fat, forty and female'; doubts have been cast on this medical aphorism, but it should be encouraging to women who are moderate wine drinkers that their chance of developing gallstones is 40 per cent less than that of abstainers.

When stones do form in the gall bladder of a spirit drinker of either sex, they are more likely to be related to the sugary drinks used as mixers than to the alcoholic base. Research has also shown that there is no loss of function of the gall bladder even in alcoholics, and that large doses of alcohol actually improve it.

Alcohol can have an immediate effect on the large bowel because it is capable of inducing a gastro-colic reflex. This reflex causes motility in the large gut when the stomach is either distended or irritated by food. It was much valued by our Victorian forebears, who prided themselves on the effect breakfast had on the regularity of their bowels. This reaction of the large bowel may also be observed in restaurants where business deals are done. The tension of negotiations, coupled with rich food and heavy wine, can be too much for many people's stomachs; the gastro-colic reflex is stimulated and the strong cup of black coffee at the end of the meal often precipitates a quick rush from the room.

This problem of over-sensitive guts often afflicts people with irritable bowel syndrome if they drink alcohol: particularly if they are tense, they are liable to suffer from wind and intestinal hurry. Whereas in most situations where the health of a person is adversely affected by alcohol it is the amount consumed that determines the response, in irritable bowel syndrome, as in migraine and headaches, the type of alcohol is important. Most sufferers from the syndrome find that the darker the drink, the greater the effect on the guts. Port, brandy, whisky, rum, red wine and beer all seem to have a greater laxative effect than white wine and clear spirits.

In *The Anatomy of Melancholy*, written in the seventeenth century, Robert Burton was almost certainly describing irritable bowel syndrome when he wrote of how some drinks can produce wind. Burton described cider and perry as 'windy drinks' and goes on to express his amazement that:

> Yet in some shires of England, normally in France and Guipusca in Spain 'tis their common drink and they are no wit offended with it.

In the rather more sophisticated twentieth century, excessive wind can be a cause of social embarrassment, as there is not always a convenient dog in the drawing room which can be blamed. The most common reason for a visit to the gastroenterologist at the local hospital is still irritable bowel syndrome, and many of the luckless victims of this complaint find they have to be careful about the number and type of drinks taken.

Conversely, red wine can sometimes be helpful in cases where the diarrhoea is due to bacterial or viral pathogens (organisms which cause disease). The French traditionally believe that claret or Beaujolais are the wines of choice for those suffering from the sort of mild food poisoning – 'traveller's diarrhoea' – sometimes caught in restaurants overseas when the diner is not immune to the prevailing organisms. A report by a team of American doctors in the *British Medical Journal* for December 1995 suggested that even diluted wine may be enough to protect the unwary traveller from the adverse effects of pathogenic E coli, salmonella and shigella (a cause of dysentery).

Modern American science was only confirming the beneficial effects of wine on a troubled intestine that has been observed down the centuries. Bordeaux was prescribed for cholera victims in 1822 and 1886 and seems to have had some benefit, thereby confirming the French faith in its powers. On other occasions, public health doctors have suggested adding wine to water known to be polluted in the hope that it might prevent infection. Professor Rambuteau advocated this extravagant step as a prophylactic to rid France of cholera in the nineteenth century, and the Viennese physician Pieck showed that the addition of wine to polluted water resulted in a mixture that was safe (if not particularly inviting) to drink.

The entire digestive tract, mouth to anus, is sensitive to stimulation by alcohol: the mouth can become abnormally dry, and many patients swear that certain drinks make their haemorrhoids worse. However, the gastro-intestinal tract is capable of developing true physiological tolerance to the stimulatory effects of drinking, and therefore if the alcohol is suddenly left off, it may, like the central nervous system when deprived of a drug, demonstrate withdrawal symptoms. These can range from delayed gastric emptying and constipation on the one hand to a heightened gastro-colic reflex and diarrhoea on the other. The mechanism of these withdrawal symptoms is not fully understood, and the response varies from person to person.

Although doctors argue over the mechanism by which alcohol alters gastric and intestinal motility, the lay public have no doubt about the fact that over-indulgence causes trouble with their stomach and guts the next day. This too has been known since Roman days: many paintings from this period graphically portray the nausea and vomiting which can follow excessive consumption of food and wine. Modern science, however, has provided the evidence to support the time-honoured belief that a small amount of alcohol improves digestion.

Despite the support of physiologists and food scientists, the custom of the pre-dinner drink is unfortunately not always observed; people now take pride in saying, 'I never drink before meals,' as if this were praiseworthy. They may be sacrificing their digestion to such ill-advised principles. Scientific evidence demonstrates that wine and beer increase gastrin production.

The value of alcohol as an aid to digestion was summed up by Hippocrates:

Wine in itself is a remedy; it nourishes the blood of man, it delights the stomach and soothes care and affliction.

Most modern doctors would agree.

7

Effects of alcohol

A glass of beer, wine or spirits provides calories – alcohol is capable of oxidation just like any other foodstuff – but the well-orientated rarely take it instead of a meal, but because of its taste and its effect on the higher centres of the brain.

HALT ('hungry, angry, lonely and tired') is the acronym taught to heavy drinkers to warn them about the state of mind which may tempt them to return to drinking after they have been 'dried out'. These same feelings, which experience shows to be a sometimes impossible hurdle for those who have given up drinking, also sum up the advantages of alcohol. An alcoholic drink, because it dulls those parts of the brain which respond to the stresses and strains of life, enables the weary worker to shrug off the worries of the day and concentrate on his family.

This relaxing effect of alcohol on the higher nervous centres induces a sense of well-being, lubricating social intercourse, making conversation hum, lowering inhibitions and increasing extroversion. It is therefore for very good reasons that, certainly for several thousand years, alcohol has been served at all celebratory and festive occasions.

The original settlers in the United States, although usually of Puritan or Nonconformist origins, had no inhibitions about drinking. These early colonists, like those in Australia, regarded alcohol as a health-giving food. They also understood its calming effect on the local labour: it could be used to pacify the native Indians, who took to alcohol all too readily, and also proved useful on the plantations as a means of encouraging the slaves to work harder and accept their lot. Likewise, over one hundred years later American trade union leaders supported prohibition because alcohol quenched the fire in the belly of the workers and

took away their desire to join the unions and confront the bosses.

The oxidation of 1 gram of alcohol produces 7 kilocalories of energy. It is oxidized at a constant rate by each individual, but the rate does vary from person to person: it becomes faster in the heavy drinker, provided their liver has been able to take the strain without becoming diseased. The standard teaching is that someone who has become tolerant to alcohol through regular use metabolizes alcohol 25 per cent more quickly than the teetotaller who has been given a glass of brandy for medicinal reasons. Recent research suggests that the figure of 25 per cent is an underestimate and that 33 per cent is more likely. However, the ability of regular drinkers to hold their alcohol is not in the main the result of faster metabolism, but because all the tissues can develop a tolerance to alcohol.

Blood levels of alcohol that would make some people incapable have little effect on those used to drinking. When I was MP for Norwich South, a politician as well known for his drinking as for his sagacity kindly came to speak in support of my campaign. Knowing his habits, we had put two very strong gins and tonic by the door leading to the hall in which he was to speak. The minister, knowing full well that I knew he liked to be 'primed', held out his hand for a glass before he went to meet the masses – and then held out his hand again.

Before he spoke he had drunk seven double gins and tonic, but he did not show, even to a knowing and questing medical eye, any ill effects. The minister made a brilliant speech, and enjoyed dinner and some of our better claret afterwards, before being driven home quite in control of his faculties. He did not only metabolize his alcohol quickly; his brain was used to its effect, and his personality was such that inhibitions which would be eroded in a lesser man were kept tightly reined in. This gin-drinking politician was following in the footsteps of a greater statesman: in the days when Winston Churchill earned most of his income from lecturing and writing, it was part of his contract that the remuneration should include a bottle of champagne, which had to be served before his lecture.

Contrary to the standard teaching, recent research has shown that experienced drinkers whose metabolic processes have not been destroyed by excessive consumption deal with their alcohol up to one-third, rather than one-quarter, faster than the occasional drinker. Once the liver has been damaged, however, even a glass or two, particularly if taken on an empty stomach, can produce all the signs of intoxication. This was always Lord George Brown's defence for his public humiliations. I did not believe that the former Foreign Secretary was being entirely accurate until I was with him on a formal occasion and saw his demeanour change from that of a thoughtful elder statesman to an aggressive and churlish drunk after a couple of drinks.

As we have seen, alcohol is absorbed from both the gastro-intestinal tract and the stomach, but the rate of absorption is very much faster in the small intestine. Anything that keeps the alcohol in the stomach is therefore likely to reduce the speed at which its influence becomes apparent.

The most dangerous drinks are those where spirits are diluted with a mixer to give an alcoholic strength of between 15 and 30 per cent by volume. If the mixers are bland, the combined drink still has a hefty kick, but not so hefty that the pylorus closes – as it would do if neat spirits were taken. Examples of drinks of this particularly intoxicating strength include vodka mixed with fruit juices, champagne cocktails, or even that 1930s favourite the White Lady, a pulverizing combination of gin, cointreau and lemon. Some combinations taste so affable and refreshing that they give the illusion the drinker is taking something no stronger than lemonade. The old ditty that warned of the dangers of cocktails is as apposite now as it was forty years ago:

> Beware of the wily Martini
> And don't exceed two at the most
> With three you'll be under the table
> With four you'll be under the host.

Alcohol is metabolized by the enzyme alcohol dehydrogenase (ADH) in the stomach, but only in very small quantities: the majority of the processing takes place in the liver. A small proportion of the alcohol is also excreted in the breath and the urine, which has little influence on the speed at which the drinker sobers up, but has proved an invaluable aid to police forces throughout the world who need to operate breathalysers or collect confirmatory samples.

The ADH converts alcohol to acetaldehyde, which is then further oxidized to acetate. There is a subsidiary system, known as the microsomal ethanol oxidizing system, that also metabolizes alcohol: it is probably this which is stimulated to greater efficiency by the regular consumption of alcohol and gives the hardened drinker his 'head for liquor'.

ADH is polymorphic: it exists in different forms in different species. By an amazing quirk of nature, the enzyme system that breaks down alcohol in Oriental peoples is different from that in Europeans, and indeed in most other ethnic groups. When drinking alcohol, Chinese and Japanese people flush very readily and their faces become suffused. Though this difference may be uncomfortable it does not alter the nature of the hangover – but it betrays the way in which they spent their evening when they return home. It has certainly not deterred the Chinese from drinking: since 1991, when Western influences were becoming widespread, the consumption of beer has more than doubled and that of spirits has doubled, whereas that of wine – the Chinese have always been wine drinkers – has only risen by a comparatively modest 20 per cent.

When oxidized by the microsomal ethanol oxidizing system, alcohol only provides two-thirds of the calories it does when oxidized by ADH. The relative proportions of alcohol oxidized by the two systems is unknown, but this may partly account for the fact that some regular drinkers gain less weight than would be expected. In excessive drinkers, however, malabsorption and changes in liver function are very much more important factors in this phenomenon.

Every year, particularly in the autumn term, when a new intake is entering the universities, there are media stories of sudden death from acute alcohol poisoning. Young people carefully brought up in homes where a drink was only offered at Christmas and birthdays suddenly find themselves let loose in the students' union bar. It is a frightening sight. Freed from the constraints of well-meaning parental control, they are quite unprepared to face the temptations of an independent life. Eighteen-year-olds will drink ten pints in a session – and unlike the rest of the adult population, students are just as likely to drink the bar dry on a Wednesday lunchtime as on a Saturday evening.

Gross binge drinking can kill. Even hardened but unwise journalists have been known to die from it after press receptions. One respected correspondent went to a conference, accepted the proffered hospitality too readily, and retired to the lavatory. When the time came for his colleagues to leave, they looked for him, received no response to their anxious knocks on the door, forced an entry and found he had died.

Cause of death was described as 'swallowing his own tongue', a simplistic way of describing the effect of the relaxation, and therefore obstruction, of the airways due to inhibition of the medullary centres of the brain. More commonly – and sometimes at a slightly lower blood alcohol level – people suffering from acute alcohol poisoning drown in their own vomit, as the reflex centres in the brain that normally prevent this by making the person cough and splutter are anaesthetized by the alcohol.

At 30 mg of alcohol per 100 ml of blood, the effect of two drinks (British units), there may be some increased liability to accident, but in most cases the drinker will feel in total possession of their faculties, relaxed without being elated. If there has been any effect on their intellect, it has probably been to sharpen it. But although the levels at which alcohol takes effect vary enormously, for the average light to moderate drinker the road after this is all downhill.

At 50 mg per 100 ml, or three units (three half pints of beer, about three glasses of wine or just three pub tots of spirits), the drinker is becoming obviously cheerful: inhibitions may be loosened and judgement may not be quite as astute as normal. At 80 mg (after five standard pub drinks) comes the point at which one's driving is considered to be impaired and therefore a danger to oneself and other road users.

At 150 mg (ten drinks) the drinker is beginning to lose self-control, to the point where they would not be able to convince their great-aunt or the local parson that they were totally sober. There will be some loss of control over the emotions, the voice might be slightly slurred, and the drinker's true personality might be displayed. The laid-back and jolly could become exuberant, the kindly might slide into the maudlin, and the tense or aggressive could become quarrelsome. *In vino veritas*: those who by a huge effort of will have for years deluded their friends into thinking they were amiable may suddenly be exposed in their true light as aggressive and two-faced.

By the time they have had twelve drinks, the drinker is staggering, vision is blurred and the memory of the night's events will be none too clear the next morning. Almost double that amount to twenty-two drinks and there is oblivion: the blood alcohol level is at 400 mg per 100 ml, the drinker is difficult to

" I KNOW - I'LL SAY IT WASN'T ME DRIVING ! "

rouse and has no concept of what is going on around them. If they then take another eight drinks before lapsing into coma, they might never come round; anyone fool enough to take thirty drinks in an evening would be very lucky to wake up. These are the figures offered by the Royal College of Physicians.

Those who can do even simple arithmetic might at first sight be puzzled by these figures, but it should be understood that during an evening's drinking the body is hard at work metabolizing the alcohol already absorbed.

Not even the Glasgow University champion drinker can down his pints so quickly that there is not time for a few units to have been processed before he has finished his evening's drinking. It is difficult to account for the interesting clinical observation that the same blood alcohol level achieved when a drinker is becoming intoxicated is more physically and mentally disabling than it is when the same person is sobering up. This is known as the 'Mellanby Effect' and may demonstrate that the human body is able to develop immediate tolerance to the ill-effects of alcohol. Others feel that it may just be a reflection of the differing environments in which the drinkers are likely to find themselves during the course of the night: when sobering up, they are more likely to be alone and tired – and there will be no party spirit.

The average person's metabolic system clears the blood of

alcohol at the rate of 15 mg per 100 ml of blood every hour: a very easy figure to remember, as it means that one unit, the equivalent of a glass of wine, is detoxified hourly. The rate at which oxidization takes place is independent of the amount drunk. This has important medico-legal implications, as it means that the person who has been drinking heavily into the small hours may still be under the influence, and over the limit for driving, next morning. It only requires a couple of gin and tonics before a rather late dinner, a bottle of wine with the meal and two glasses of brandy afterwards for one still to have an appreciable quantity of alcohol circulating in the blood on the way to work.

Medical students have always remembered the various stages of drunkenness by reference to pairs of words beginning with D. The first stage is 'Dry and Decent', followed in turn by 'Delighted and Devilish', 'Delinquent and Disgusting', 'Dizzy and Delirious', 'Dazed and Dejected' and finally 'Dead Drunk'. Any casualty officer will know that this last is not just a meaningless alliteration: there is not one who will not have battled to save the life of the man or woman admitted 'Dead Drunk' and few who will not remember cases where a patient has been brought in dead.

Older generations not in the medical profession used to plot the downhill course of an evening's excessive drinking in terms of the 'Seven Oses'. First the potential drunk becomes 'Verbose', then 'Amorous', followed by 'Grandiose'. As the night wears on, the 'Grandiose' King of the Bar lapses into the 'Morose'. Before the end of the evening he is more than sorry for himself and slides into the 'Lachrymose' before ending up 'Comatose'.

Even the most sensible drinker is likely to have tripped up at some time or another and experienced a hangover. Even the lightest of social drinkers, who may never have personally experienced a hangover, will have seen others who have not felt too well at breakfast, and will know the symptoms: headaches, irritability, depression, sweating, nausea, an upset gut, even a shake, are the penalties for excessive drinking. The unjustness of the hangover is that the body is a very unfair judge: some drinkers are sentenced to a day's misery for drinking only half a bottle of wine, whereas others can have three times the amount without suffering.

Intoxication and the ill-effects of long-term drinking are both dependent upon the amount of alcohol drunk. It does not matter whether the drinks are made from the grape or the grain (or are a mixture of both), whether the wine is red or white, good or bad: the drinker gets drunk because he has taken too much alcohol. Hangovers are different, however. The severity of the hangover – whether it is just a headache, or nausea and gastro-intestinal upset as well – is dependent on the nature of the drink as well as on the quantity drunk. The old advice about not mixing drinks will not stop anyone from becoming as drunk as a lord, but it may stop them from being sick during the night or having a splitting headache the next day.

The hangover is in part due to the acetaldehyde circulating as a result of the metabolism of the alcohol and in part due to the congeners, organic chemicals which exist in all drinks and give them their characteristic colour and taste. Although it has been shown that dark drinks are no more noxious in the long term than light ones, everybody who has ever been into a bar knows that brandy is more likely to cause a hangover than whisky and that vodka is more benign than either; in addition, too much port can be more crippling the next day than too much dry sherry. One reason for the switch in public taste from brandy to whisky may be that whisky has fewer congeners and is therefore less likely to cause a hangover.

When the congeners are processed by the body, the resulting products include methanol, wood alcohol, which in its turn is metabolized to formic acid, which gives ants their sting, and formaldehyde, the toxic chemical known to every embryo biologist and strong enough to preserve even Damien Hirst's artistic dissections. Not surprisingly, these products are not kind to the brain cells: the drinker develops a severe headache and feels weary and irritable. Unwise drinkers will also be lucky if they escape gastro-intestinal problems.

Dr Ian Calder, a consultant at the National Hospital for

Neurology and Neurosurgery in London, has suggested in the *British Medical Journal* that hangovers are worse in people who become angry or depressed, are neurotic or have had stressful life events in the previous year. Dr Calder may well be right: when I was a political candidate for the Isle of Ely, a famously hard-drinking area, I kept a note of how I felt the morning after a meeting. I discovered that my hangover (I was still young enough to have them in those days) was far more related to any tensions or stress during the evening meeting than to either the amount or the type of alcohol. If the meeting went well, I was headache-free the next day.

Alcohol dries the mouth by inhibiting the production of saliva and dehydrates the whole body – except for the brain, which swells. The dehydration is the result of the diuretic effect of alcohol on the kidneys; it causes them to excrete more water, hence the urine is pale, dilute and plentiful. The brain swells despite the general dehydration because of the damage done to the nervous tissue, which in consequence becomes oedematous, waterlogged. There are a few advantages to growing old: one of them is that hangovers are less likely, and above all, the headaches induced by heavy drinking are only a memory. Even the brain of a President of the Royal Society shrivels with age and no longer fits the presidential skull so snugly; there is room for expansion, so the nervous tissue does not become compressed.

The depression and irritability experienced after drinking is mainly a result of temporary cerebral damage, but hypoglycaemia, abnormally low blood sugar, also plays a part. This accounts for the heavy sweating after drinking, despite the dehydration; it also contributes to the headache and is partly responsible for the dizziness, weakness of the limbs and blurred vision. The hypoglycaemia during a hangover stems from two causes: the liver's ability to release sugar into the bloodstream is inhibited, and the pancreas becomes more efficient at producing the insulin which reduces blood sugar levels. In adults, the low blood sugar is tiresome and contributes to the unpleasantness of the hangover, but is unlikely to do any lasting damage.

To treat a hangover each symptom needs individual treatment. On going to bed, the heavy drinker should drink a pint or two of water, which will reduce the dehydration. Some Alka Seltzer at the same time may settle the stomach and pre-empt the headache. It is as well to have some water by the bed too, so that when the drunkard's 'false dawn' breaks at two o'clock in the morning and the partygoer awakes hot, sweaty, sleepless and parched, they can quench their thirst with another couple of pints.

Next morning, each symptom has to be treated step by step. An effervescent headache cure, which now usually contains paracetamol rather than aspirin, is the best, as it is less likely to increase inflammation of the gastric mucosa. Some doctors prefer a non-steroidal anti-inflammatory agent, such as ibuprofen, which suppresses prostaglandins. It is even better to take the paracetamol or ibuprofen with the water before going to bed. If there is a pressing engagement early in the morning, an anti-diarrhoeal preparation – such as Imodium, which may be obtained over the counter, or Lomotil, for which a prescription is needed – may make it possible to attend the meeting without an ignominious flight from the office. Not much can be done about the wind, for who takes charcoal biscuits to a lunch party?

For the hypoglycaemia which is an important ingredient of any hangover, the cure is obvious but sometimes difficult to put into practice. The tough old trooper who says, 'What you need, my boy, is a breakfast of bacon and eggs,' does not understand that, although his advice is physiologically sound, the thought of bacon and eggs, let alone their congealing presence on the breakfast plate, might convert one's nausea into vomiting. If the slightly hungover can enjoy a hearty breakfast, life will be better thereafter, as the blood sugar will rise. Coffee is a hallowed cure, and may certainly restore morale after a disturbed night. Unfortunately, it will not improve the digestive tract: it increases the gastro-intestinal motility, which may precipitate a rush to the lavatory. Furthermore, it will act as a diuretic and in so doing increase the dehydration. Coffee does not help the unwise drinker to sober up after a heavy drinking session.

The 'hair of the dog' – a drink to settle the stomach and get rid of the headache – is another time-honoured remedy. It may come in the form of a chemist's pick-me-up or the barman's personal remedy, or others may just prefer to order themselves a Bloody Mary. The idea of the 'hair of the dog' has always been frowned upon as a possible first step down the slippery slope to alcoholism. This remedy does in fact work, as the alcohol interferes with the metabolism of the congeners to formaldehyde and then to formic acid.

The Prairie Oyster, a rather daunting mixture of pepper, egg yolks and tomato juice made brown with Worcester sauce, counteracts the low blood sugar. The Morning Cocktail, fruit juice sweetened with honey and laced with an analgesic, usually paracetamol, also corrects the hypoglycaemia, eases the dehydration and helps the headache.

Some people swear by herbal remedies. If taken with enough fluid, they will certainly counteract the dehydration. Valerian may well be the herbal preparation of choice, as it is good for colic and spasmodic pains and helps to bring up the wind; it will also settle the nerves if they are a bit jangled after the party. The Chinese set great store by tablets containing ingredients from the Kudzo vine.

Finally, if all else fails, some people – one suspects usually men – recommend sexual intercourse the following morning. If it encourages the hungover to drop off to sleep again, it may perhaps have some curative value.

The situation is very different in children. In them, the hypoglycaemia induced by heavy drinking is not just a bearable inconvenience, but may well prove fatal. Children's brains are very sensitive to low blood sugar, and the reflexes which control breathing and the cardiovascular system can all too easily be destroyed, or the higher brain centres permanently blighted.

Small children have a strong and understandable love of copying their elders. Many a time after a party they will sneak into the room and sample drinks which have been left lying around, giggling as they taste the half-empty glasses. A small child who inadvertently becomes drunk should be taken to casualty for treatment.

One small seven- or eight-year-old, despite his parents' entreaties, was in the habit of helping himself to their drinks. One day I was telephoned by the hospital casualty unit, who said that the child had just been admitted and they suspected his comatose state was the result of a cerebral tumour; the neurosurgeon had been sent for. Knowing the child's proclivities, I suggested that it might be as well to test both blood alcohol and blood sugar levels as a preliminary precaution. Sure enough, he needed a stomach washout rather than brain surgery.

The effect of alcohol on insulin and its action on the body is perhaps part of the story of why modest drinking tends to reduce the incidence of non-insulin dependent diabetes. But it is the increasing knowledge of alcohol's influence on the cardiovascular system that has revolutionized most doctors' views about light to moderate drinking. If any anxieties remain about the desirability of a modest alcohol intake, it is only because some practitioners feel that if patients are given any encouragement to drink, an unacceptable number of them will overdo it and drink to excess.

There are many other ill effects of alcohol when taken in too large a quantity. It can, for instance, make the ears ring with tinnitus and can even cause lasting trouble with the teeth and the skin. People interested in wine, even if not expert, look at the colour of the wine in the glass, swirl it around, sniff it, and then take a sip. At a wine tasting, when there may be twenty or thirty wines to be sampled, the wine is held in the mouth and slopped around before being spat out into a bowl. The wine is ejected, not because it will make it easier to taste the next one, but in order that judgement is not blurred by inebriation. The wine taster, by sloshing the acid wine around the inside of the mouth before forcibly spitting it past the teeth, is liable to damage the teeth in the same way as bulimic patients destroy the back of their teeth. In bulimic patients the stomach acids erode the dental enamel, whereas in wine tasters it is the vinous acids. Mr Sharhid Chaudhry of Guys Hospital, London, has reported in the *British Dental Journal* on the case in which a merchant had subjected his teeth to 245,000 drenchings of wine over twenty-three years. The teeth were so worn that only the metallic fillings protruded from the gums. There is no need to give up the wine, only to clean the teeth very assiduously after a tasting.

An excessive alcohol intake over many years alters the texture of the skin. The complexion is coarsened, thread veins appear and the skin's pores become more obvious. The red-faced squire owes his countenance more to the sun, wind and lashing rain than to the contents of his sideboard, but alcohol plays some part in his appearance. Playwrights and cartoonists would find their task more difficult if they were unable to label the heavy drinkers by giving them flushed cheeks and a bulbous, pitted and acned red nose. The condition the playwright is portraying is acne rosacea. Nothing makes a sufferer from acne rosacea angrier than the assumption that the red nose is the result of an excessive alcohol intake, and the evidence is that in the majority of cases there is no link. However, anything which induces flushing exacerbates acne rosacea, and alcohol is no exception to this rule.

A more important effect of alcohol on the skin is its influence on psoriasis. Psoriasis is a common skin condition which affects 2 per cent of the population. It results in patches, sometimes extensive, of red raised skin covered in silvery scales. There is a strong genetic link in cases of psoriasis; however, the evidence suggests that while many patients inherit a tendency to develop the condition, other factors may be needed to trigger an actual attack. Usually the trigger which uncovers the genetic suscepti-bility remains undiscovered but it is known that emotional stress is a frequent cause. Some cases are triggered by beta blockers taken to treat high blood pressure; other patients have reacted to lithium used in the treatment of depression. Recently it has been shown that an excessive alcohol intake may also lead to psoriasis, or in existing cases make it much worse. One forty-year-old woman prided herself both on her clear skin and her ability to further her husband's ambitions by accompanying him on all his business trips and by entertaining widely for him. Suddenly she developed the most disfiguring psoriasis, not only on her body but also on her face. The patient went from dermatologist to dermatologist but none were brave enough to tell her to restrict her drinking, and my suggestions to do this were, depending on her mood, greeted with either withering scorn or a pitying smile. Finally, I persuaded her to see one of the Royal Physicians: he took one look at her, and at her liver function tests, and said, 'Mrs Wainwright, you drink too much.' Thereafter she moderated her drinking habits and her psoriasis disappeared. It is rare for psoriasis to vanish entirely in this way, although it frequently waxes and wanes. In heavy drinkers it tends to affect principally the soles and palms of the feet and hands, and skin creases. The skin lesions are very inflamed in psoriasis related to alcohol, but show less scaling than in other cases.

It is estimated that in up to a third of patients with psoriasis there may be an association with heavy drinking, but interestingly the alcohol dependence in patients with this condition is unusually rare.

The Medical Council on Alcoholism, which has drawn doctors' attention to the link between alcohol and psoriasis, has also exposed another association between heavy drinking and skin troubles. There is a connection between discoid eczema, the round patches of eczema characteristically seen on the shins of middle aged men, and over-indulgence. Frequently, these patches only respond to treatment once the sufferer has modified his alcohol intake.

8

Alcohol and the liver

Nine-tenths of the alcohol drunk is processed by the liver. The principal enzyme involved in its metabolism is alcohol dehydrogenase, although other microsomal enzymes are also present. Part of the metabolic process is the production of acetaldehyde, a highly toxic substance which contributes to hangovers and in the long term causes liver damage.

Doctors do not agree about the degree of hazard that alcohol represents to the liver, but it is certain that there *is* a hazard and that the incidence of cirrhosis of the liver is increasing in the Western world. Some of this increase may be more apparent than real, as doctors are now more prepared to enter cirrhosis of the liver as a cause of death on the death certificate.

Previously, great efforts were made to spare relatives the thought that the death could have been induced by life-style, but it is now generally accepted by the lay public as well as doctors that although alcohol is a very important cause of cirrhosis, there are others. Until comparatively recently, an inquest had to be held if cirrhosis was thought to be the cause of death – another reason why the entry was often omitted.

The *Oxford Textbook of Medicine* suggests that 80 gm of alcohol (eight or nine drinks) taken daily by a man, or 50 gm a day (five or six drinks) taken by a woman, gives the drinker a 15 per cent chance of developing liver damage. The Americans are rather more pessimistic: their standard medical textbook suggests that about three-fifths of this figure for men and half for women could be enough to cause damage.

All the experts agree, however, that the consumption has to be regular and spread over many years. You would be unlucky to develop cirrhosis in under fifteen years of regular heavy drinking. The neo-prohibitionists will contend that there is no such thing as a 'safe' level of alcohol intake. This is undoubtedly true – and it is equally true that guidelines for living cannot be based on a tiny (and ill-defined) minority who, it is presumed, have a highly unusual, if not aberrant, metabolic system.

The exact proportion of drinkers who will develop cirrhosis is also disputed. Forty years ago, when I was a student, we were taught that a third of heavy drinkers would develop the condition if they failed to modify their habits. Later, this figure was reduced to one in five, and now it is almost one in seven, with a standard American textbook quoting one in ten. This lengthening of the odds on developing cirrhosis may reflect improved diagnosis, but it also is a result of doctors understanding that liver disease is often the result of many different factors.

Many alcoholics are malnourished. They drink well but eat badly. The determined nutritionists who write in popular magazines reserve their most savage condemnation for what they term 'empty calories'. As we know, the calories provided by wine and other drinks are not entirely empty, because they provide flavonoids and other trace elements as energy, but compared to some foods it would perhaps be fair to say that they are 'relatively empty'.

A heavy drinker may therefore satisfy his hunger without taking in all the essential nutrients the body needs to remain in peak

THE ROAD TO RUIN

condition. The situation is made worse by the fact that alcohol in excess can have a deleterious effect on the organs of digestion and on the absorption of food through the gut wall into the bloodstream.

There is a popular myth that all cirrhosis is the result of over-indulgence in alcohol. This is quite untrue: many cases follow hepatitis in early life and others are secondary to heart disease. In any small community, the diagnosis of cirrhosis is often greeted with sidelong glances and a knowing smirk. Even the most rabid teetotaller can – and often does, if he or she was born in a country where hepatitis B is endemic – suffer from cirrhosis.

Although those who drink very heavily may only have one chance in ten of developing cirrhosis of the liver, they should not become complacent. Cirrhosis is not the only liver disease which afflicts the heavy drinker: the potential damage encompasses a wide spectrum from a little fatty infiltration to cancer of the liver. Although the drinker may not suffer any lasting damage, the skilled pathologist can detect the very first signs of potential liver damage after a month or so of heavy drinking, by studying microscopic slides prepared from liver biopsy specimens. In a small minority of people who have drunk to excess for many years, alcohol *can* lead to cirrhosis, and in time this cirrhosis leads to primary cancer of the liver. Once again, malnutrition may be a factor in the development of both cirrhosis and cancer of the liver.

It is said that between the wars, when there was under-nourishment in those city areas where unemployment was rife, cirrhosis was commonly found amongst the clergy; they had little money and a stressful life, so the temptation for the struggling incumbent was to spend the money on alcohol rather than protein. Those who are well nourished should not be complacent for, contrary to medical teaching in the past, liver damage can occur even in those who eat well and are not malnourished.

There are other causes of fatty livers apart from over-indulgence in alcohol; fortunately, whatever the cause, these conditions are usually reversible and are not an inevitable forerunner of cirrhosis. Men who become abstinent, or even cut back their drinking to sensible levels, find that their livers regenerate. As a result of hormonal differences, however, when women stop drinking once liver damage had been detected and thereafter change their drinking pattern, their recovery rate is not as high as it is in men, and the liver changes may be progressive.

In patients who show evidence of fatty infiltration, the liver will be swollen and tender and they will complain of loss of appetite and nausea. The nausea is particularly troublesome early in the morning, so when a middle-aged heavy drinker complains of symptoms similar to those of a young woman during early pregnancy a question or two about his drinking habits is usually pertinent.

In a proportion of cases, fatty infiltration later leads to cirrhosis. This progression takes time, and it is therefore unusual to find a patient with alcoholic cirrhosis before late middle age. Because of the difference in their life-style and drinking habits, the incidence of alcoholic liver disease is higher in men than in women, but notwithstanding this, women are drink for drink more likely to fall prey to it because they are less able to metabolize alcohol.

Many people are unaware that they have cirrhosis, but even these asymptomatic cases are usually conscious of the fact that they are drinking too much and are at risk. Patients who do have specific symptoms will complain of general tiredness, weakness, swollen feet and weight loss. The weakness, secondary to muscle wasting, is a very striking feature. Even the pub arm-wrestling champion will lose his crown if he drinks too much. After taking ten pints a night for fifteen years, the strongest man's arm muscles may be so weakened by the alcohol that he could be pushed over by a ten-stone weakling.

The person with advanced cirrhosis, and therefore severe liver failure, will show all or many of the usual symptoms. He – it is more often a man – will have spider naevi, large breasts, testicular atrophy, pink palms and chipmunk's cheeks (from the enlarged parotids), and in both sexes the body hair will be sparse. In terminal liver disease, the patients become jaundiced, the weight loss is extreme, their limbs become spindly, their abdomens swell and they develop various neurological signs and symptoms.

For the heavy drinker, the progression from fatty infiltration to liver failure via cirrhosis is not the only route to liver disease: it can also occur as the result of alcoholic hepatitis. After a night's binge drinking, alcoholic hepatitis can occur in people of any age, even those who have previously been very modest in their intake. Conversely, it is also found after prolonged drinking.

One middle-aged man beat the male menopause by moving from being chairman of an industrial company to being head of a media organization. Soon after his move, he developed palpitations and breathlessness; on examination, he had a rapid, irregularly irregular heartbeat and the ECG confirmed that he was fibrillating. No sooner had his cardiac rhythm been restored than he was back again complaining of upper right abdominal pain, tenderness and minimal jaundice.

Tests showed that he was suffering from alcoholic hepatitis. The change in his wining and dining habits that marked his translation from the prosaic company boardroom to the glamour of the television world had been too much for him, and he had developed acute signs of over-indulgence in both his cardiovascular system and his liver.

The severity of alcoholic hepatitis varies enormously. Some people only have a slightly tender upper right abdomen, coupled with rather more nausea than they feel they deserve after the night's excesses. Others go on to develop acute liver failure. Professor Stephen White in his book *Russia Goes Dry* quotes many dramatic stories of heavy binge drinking in Russia which cause the authorities great consternation. Life expectancy is falling rapidly in Russia; although this is probably for a variety of reasons, alcoholism is among the principal factors and has received much of the blame.

The good news is that many patients who develop liver failure as a result of cirrhosis caused by heavy drinking do very well after a liver transplant. The overwhelming majority (over 90 per cent) of those who have a transplant give up drinking in excess – but interestingly, most remain light to moderate drinkers.

Liver Cirrhosis Mortality and Alcohol Consumption, Selected Countries mid 1970s

From Office of Health Economics. Alcohol Reducing the Harm, 1981

Country	Change in alcohol consumption since 1950–52
Iceland	+236%
Norway	+105%
Sweden	+48%
Finland	+191%
England & Wales	+74%
Poland	165%
Hollard	+337%
Germany DR	+337%
Yugoslavia	+230%
Denmark	+130%
Czechoslovakia	+88%
Belgium	+55%
Switzerland	+56%
Hungary	+123%
Austria	+107%
Germany FR	+247%
Spain	+73%
France	-6%

Cirrhosis of liver

Alcohol consumption

9

Gout

Almost two men in every hundred suffer from gout, which makes it the most common of the inflammatory arthritic conditions. The condition owes its fame not to its prevalence, but to its association with drinking, and this makes it a regular topic of conversation whenever men over the age of eighteen gather together. Gout is much more common in the male and it is rare before late adolescence.

Long before Dr Garrod, the eminent Victorian physician who made a speciality of gout, described its features in scientific terms, other doctors had their own views as to how it should be treated. Only sixty years before Garrod published his seminal work, the medical profession was still recommending that a gouty limb should be rubbed with warm treacle and then bound with flannel.

If this did not cure the patient, a textbook by John Wesley, a physician and not the preacher, had a simpler remedy: to undress at six o'clock in the evening, wrap oneself up in blankets, soak one's legs in hot water, then suddenly freeze them with a good douche from a bucket of cold water drawn directly from the well. Thereafter the gouty patient had to climb into a warm bed and sweat profusely until the morning.

Dr Garrod was firm in his belief in the close association between gout and alcohol:

> The use of fermented or alcoholic liquors is the most powerful of all predisposing causes of gout.

Garrod was, however, perpetuating a view that is so simplistic as to be misleading. Gout is an arthritic disease that afflicts those with high levels of uric acid circulating in their blood. In some –

but not all – such people, urate crystals are deposited in connective tissue, which then stimulates what one doctor describes as an 'acute inflammatory reaction' but which to the patient is simply an agonizing and inflamed joint. The traditional view of gout is nowhere better illustrated than in the nineteenth-century cartoons from *Punch*, where the elderly, ruddy-faced, plethoric man sits in his chair with his feet on the gout stool and the brandy on the table beside him

Gout is not exclusively a penalty paid for over-indulgence. The factors which precipitate an attack are far more complex, but what *is* certain is that the form in which the alcohol is taken is not one of them – despite the advice of Louis XIV's doctor that champagne should be substituted for burgundy at court dinners. The view of gout expressed by *Punch*, Dr Garrod and the French royal doctor is particularly unfair to modest drinkers, who may also suffer from the condition. Garrod's assertion that drinking alcohol is the basic cause of gout is now known to be scientifically incorrect. The underlying cause is not the bottle, but a raised uric acid level. People with this biochemical abnormality may have symptom-free lives for many years.

The doctor has a duty to determine which of numerous factors has triggered a particular attack of gout. The immediate cause in someone who normally has a raised uric acid level can be gluttony, excessive dieting, an unwise choice of food, lead poisoning, taking diuretic pills, injury or surgery to the joint, or an infection totally unrelated to the joints – as well as, of course, an excessive alcohol intake. Overweight people are more likely to suffer from gout than those whose weight is within the approved range for their height and build. Some drugs, including aspirin when taken in small doses (but surprisingly not after a large dose), can also be the cause of a sudden attack

However, there is no surer way of precipitating gout in someone with a raised serum uric acid level than for them to go without breakfast and an adequate lunch, but still to find time to attend a drinks party on the way home to supper. Excessive alcohol may be only one of many ways of triggering an attack of acute gout, but it is a 'particularly potent' one (to quote Dr Garrod) when combined with a crash diet and subsequent hours of starvation. In the long term, what is important is to find the risk factors for those with a raised serum uric acid.

The story is told of one patient in the nineteenth century who was recommended by his doctor to avoid brown sweet sherry, as this caused acute joint pains within a few hours; it was suggested that he should take something lighter. His wine merchant, after much thought, sent the patient some Manzanilla, but it was returned with a polite note, saying that the drinker preferred to risk the gout.

A raised uric acid level is in most cases inherited. Thus the greatest risk factor in the development of gout is to have fore-bears who also suffered from it. Obesity is another important fac-tor when the weight gain has occurred early in adult life or if the patient has diabetes, a high blood cholesterol and a raised blood pressure. Doctors can unwittingly make attacks of gout more likely by treating hypertension with diuretics, the so-called 'water pills', as these increase the level of uric acid in the blood.

The association between gout and alcohol is so firmly fixed in people's minds that many other causes of the condition must have been under-treated. Patients have had to suffer heavy humour, together with advice to drink less, when what they really needed is some basic treatment. Refusing the second glass of wine and avoiding shellfish, liver, kidneys and other foods rich in purines – nitrogenous compounds produced by the metabolism of certain proteins and liable to precipitate gout – may display admirable self-control, but will ultimately prove inadequate to treat this biochemical disease, of which a gouty joint is the most obvious sign.

Contrary to popular mythology, gout does not only affect port-loving squires. Port does, of course, contain alcohol, but there is no evidence that it is any more likely to cause an attack than any other alcoholic drink, including white wine and spirits. If any drink is more likely to cause gout than another, it is beer, which contains a high level of purines.

Gout can attack the abstemious as well as the drunkard. Puritans in the seventeenth century were not, as one might have learnt in fourth-form history classes, all teetotallers, but their life-style was ordered and over-indulgence would have been unthinkable; even so, gout was recorded amongst Cromwell's troops.

The disciplined non-drinker who mocks gout sufferers should remember the plight of John Milton, one of the best-known historical figures to have suffered from this disease. Milton had no doubt about the agony of an attack of gout, as he suffered from it during the greater part of his life. The pain he endured is said to have served as his inspiration for *Paradise Lost*. In later life Milton not only went blind but also had hands grotesquely deformed by gouty arthritis, which left his joints twisted and gnarled from the deposition of chalky tophi disfiguring the skin around the joints.

Despite his disabilities, Milton continued to write, but his life, which had been so varied in his earlier years – including extensive travelling on the Continent and his activities as a keen Parliamentarian during the Civil War – inevitably became constrained. His financial position never recovered from the Restoration, when he agreed to accept a fine rather than continuing imprisonment, and he died at the age of sixty-six. Doctors gave the cause of death as gout.

Doctors had been aware of gout for centuries before Milton's death, but the first careful scientific account of it was given by Dr Thomas Sydenham in 1683, nineteen years after the poet had been buried alongside his father in St Giles Cripplegate. Sydenham had had as interesting an early career as Milton; his life in Oxford was interrupted by the onset of the Civil War, in which he fought with distinction alongside his brothers on the side of Parliament. After the war, Sydenham returned to Oxford, qualified as a doctor, became a Fellow of All Souls, but then abandoned his medical vocation to become a professional cavalry officer.

Sydenham flourished in the army and fought bravely in various campaigns, but when his fighting days were over he returned to medicine and this time studied in France. He soon became a physician as well-regarded on the Continent as he was in England.

Sydenham is now mainly remembered for his description of the symptoms of rheumatic fever and for his account of gout, in which he describes the pain, the suddenness of its onset, the extreme tenderness of the joint, the feelings of ill health, and even the slight fever sometimes associated with a classic attack of gouty arthritis. Sydenham recounted one particular symptom that patients would describe to him, and which, from my own experience, is still prevalent today: 'Doctor, my foot is so tender that I cannot bear to have the bedclothes resting on it.'

Men are eight times more likely to suffer an attack of gout than women, and it is indeed rare to diagnose the condition in a pre-menopausal woman. As in Milton's case, gout usually starts in early middle age, between thirty and sixty. In 70 per cent of cases the big toe is usually the first area to be affected, but any joint can be involved. Not infrequently, a joint damaged by trauma or some other unrelated condition will be the first to suffer an attack. Ankles, knees, wrists and elbows as well as the small joints of the hands and feet may be plagued by acute gout, and later, when the joint has been repeatedly damaged, by persistent gouty arthritis. In chronic gout the cartilage in these joints is eroded, and there are secondary hypertrophic changes which cause the deformity.

As we have seen, most people with gout can blame their ances-tors rather than their wine merchant. Genetic inheritance plays a large part in determining both purine metabolism and urate excretion, two of the main factors in determining uric acid level and hence the likelihood of gout. Not all attacks are acute: the gouty nature of transitory arthritis is often missed if the pain affects more than one joint at a time, or if it is not severe but rather an annoying discomfort. Gout also has a tendency to attack joints already damaged by other conditions. When a for-mer footballer complains of a painful, swollen knee, it is too easy to assume it is a result of injuries inflicted years earlier during some savage battle on the pitch and to forget that he might be suffering from gout. The diagnosis becomes even more difficult if previous arthroscopy and X-rays have shown osteoarthritis. Patients with transient arthritic pains are well advised to have blood tests on at least two occasions so that their uric acid levels may be estimated.

The usual pattern of gout is that after many years of a raised serum uric acid level, during which time the patient will suffer no symptoms, he (or less often she) will experience an acute attack. As time goes on, the attacks become more frequent and often more severe, and eventually a chronic arthritic condition is established, with deformed, painful joints.

The deformity of the joints is highlighted by the deposition of gouty tophi in the tissues around them. Tophi are also laid down in other cartilage such as the external ear. Urates in the form of crystals develop in the kidneys; in Britain, gout is responsible for 5 per cent of kidney stones. In this country, one in ten people who have gout also have stones, and a quarter of those will die from renal failure if the gout is not treated. In other countries, the proportion of gout sufferers who have stones is much greater: in Israel, where relatively few people drink to excess – although beer consumption per capita is higher than it is in the UK – 75 per cent of patients with gout have renal stones.

Without treatment, the stones can result in slowly progressive disease of the kidneys and eventually in possible failure; very occasionally, gout can cause acute renal failure. In the days before treatment was available, one in four severely gouty patients died from kidney failure; John Milton was one of them. In more recent times, there is the case of the splendid heavy-drinking old soldier who must also have been born with a gouty tendency, uncovered by years of service in the Mediterranean and later Africa. I first saw him when he developed kidney stones which caused a marked impairment of renal function. His treatment has dealt with the stones, his renal failure is not yet bad enough to require dramatic intervention, but although all goes well so far, one is left wishing that his biochemical abnormalities had been detected earlier. He could then have had appropriate treatment to forestall the troubles that finally overtook him.

The traditional belief that only certain types of drink precipitated an attack of gout may have its origins in the way different wines were bottled, corked and sealed in centuries gone by; the recipe used by the makers of the bottles in which the drink was stored may also have been important.

Both the seal around the cork and the glass contained high concentrations of lead. The seal would eventually disintegrate, and if the lead was not wiped away from the neck of the bottle, it could contaminate the contents when they were poured out. The longer a bottle of wine was kept, as with vintage port or claret for instance, the more likely it was that the seal would deteriorate and lead be washed into the glass. Likewise, some lead crystal decanters leached their lead into drink that was left in them for any length of time.

Chronic lead poisoning can give rise to a particular form of gout called saturnine gout – hence vintage wines, port and brandy were blamed for producing gout. Interestingly, although acute kidney failure does not usually cause attacks of gout, it does when the failure is a consequence of lead poisoning. So some of the gouty eighteenth-century squires may have been poisoned by their decanters. Thankfully, this bleak outlook for gouty patients has been revolutionized by modern pharmacy and the manufacture of safe glass and seals.

Gout is now treatable. The blood level of uric acid can be lowered by taking allopurinol, marketed as Zyloric: 300 mg a day is usually enough to stop acute gout, but some sufferers may need 600 mg or even 900 mg. However, allopurinol should not be taken for the first time during an acute attack; anti-inflammatory drugs are needed at this stage. Once the attack is well and truly over, a regular daily dose of allopurinol will in most cases keep the uric acid at a suitable level, the joints pain-free and the kidneys healthy.

When patients first take allopurinol, they may find that it actually precipitates an acute attack of gout, but a short course of anti-inflammatory drugs will usually put things right. Very occasionally, this treatment has to be continued for up to three months to prevent breakthrough attacks, but in time the transient arthritis the patient has suffered for years will be nothing but a memory.

Some patients continue to have acute attacks of gout despite adequate treatment with allopurinol. Research has shown that many of these are heavy drinkers. Unfortunately, deformed and agonizing joints do not always succeed where doctors and preachers have failed: surveys have shown that many gouty heavy drinkers refuse to change their habits. One ships' broker, witty, charming and a perfect host, resolutely refuses to modify his life-style. He finds it hard to accept that, although he never drinks to the point where he would be considered intoxicated, this can still be too much to enable the allopurinol to control his serum uric acid levels. Although he has to hobble around his Hampshire estate at weekends, his kidney function remains good and there are as yet no stones. There is some hope that he will have a long life, even if somebody else will have to fetch the bottles from the cellar.

The good news is that the same research showed allopurinol resistance to be virtually unknown in those who obeyed the Department of Health's earlier guidelines by drinking less than twenty-one units of alcohol a week. So effective is allopurinol at keeping gout at bay, even for moderate drinkers, that it has been suggested that, if the drug does not work, this may be a sign that the patient is a secret heavy drinker.

Gout is primarily a genetic biochemical problem, albeit one that might have remained undiscovered had it not been for some triggering factor. Alcohol is only one of many possible triggers, though it does seem particularly important in cases of allopurinol-resistant gout (but only if the patient drinks fairly heavily). Gouty patients taking their treatment may enjoy a glass or two of wine with the rest of us.

10

Alcohol and the brain

When David comes into the bar, a slight hush falls over the room and the groups talking to each other close ranks. Nobody wants to catch David's eye; they hope to blend into the background so that they are not singled out for his attention. David has not got halitosis, and he is not about to be banned from the premises because his feet smell. It is just that he has drunk too much for years, his brain is not what it was, his words are slurred, his memory is appalling and he will tell the same boring stories time and time again. This is David's conversational style when he is in a good mood, but if he is feeling a bit headachy, his over-emphatic opinions – usually based on not very good evidence – will silence the general chatter around him and make everybody slightly on edge in case a casual remark precipitates a diatribe.

The general public's knowledge of the effect of alcohol on the brain is based on meeting people like David, and to a lesser extent on their own experiences of a hangover. If anyone had derived their opinion solely from David's behaviour, it would be hard to convince them that alcohol in small quantities is good for the intellect and that learned neurophysiologists write papers on its advantages to cognitive function or intellectual prowess. Trouble only arises when alcohol is taken in too large quantities for too long, when someone goes on a binge, or if they have existing medical problems.

Memory lapses, known at the barside as blackouts, are an exception to this rule. Even people who only drink socially may suddenly experience a blackout, possibly after they have consumed more than usual while celebrating a special occasion. The speed at which the drinks are taken, the rate at which the alcohol is absorbed into the bloodstream and the total number of drinks taken all contribute to the likelihood of a memory lapse. Blackouts are more likely to occur if the drinker has not eaten while drinking.

One well-known and much-loved television commentator always remained suave and good company during a dinner party. He was never very interested in the food, but enjoyed his wine and almost invariably finished a couple of decanters of his host's port. The problem was that, although his behaviour was exemplary throughout the evening, when he eventually woke up the next day – sometimes not for thirty-six hours – he had no memory of the party. Although he did not regularly drink at this rate, he must have drunk enough every day to develop a very high degree of tolerance. Most people would have died from acute alcohol poisoning after a couple of bottles of port, without even taking into consideration the amount he had drunk during dinner. This popular man has now died, but he exceeded his three score years and ten.

Psychiatrists regard repeated memory lapses as a worrying symptom in people who drink. It shows that, although they may not consistently drink heavily, they are on occasions taking too much, which in time is likely to cause dependence and long-term intellectual impairment.

The advantages of moderate drinking to the mind and intellect have been analysed. According to research by C. Baum-Baicker in the mid-1980s, there are five benefits, all of which can be scientifically substantiated. Moderate drinkers:

1 Are outgoing and approach life with greater enthusiasm.
2 Suffer less stress and enjoy their professional, social and domestic life more.
3 Perform certain tasks better after a drink. (Many keyboard operators find that after a couple of drinks at lunch they can use the computer with greater dexterity. I have witnessed this myself, and similar experiments under controlled conditions have confirmed it.)
4 Have lower rates of depression, even though a hangover is

never very cheering and heavy drinking can induce long-term depression.

5 When elderly, cope better with many of the problems of age, and also seem to have better cognitive function.

" HEY – THIS PROGRAM SUDDENLY MAKES SENSE ! "

All these advantages are lost if so much alcohol has been taken that its toxic effects predominate.

The bad news is that the ability to practise some skills deteriorates after more than two drinks. Amongst these is driving, particularly if the person concerned does not drink regularly.

A person's reaction to drinking is in part determined by what they expect to happen. It is interesting that, if someone is given an alcohol-free drink which they suppose to contain alcohol, their performance deteriorates after an initial improvement, just as it would if they had really been given alcohol. The same phenomenon has been observed amongst partygoers, who were able to get into the festive mood even though their drink did not contain the alcohol they expected.

Although heavy alcohol consumption is accompanied by intellectual deterioration – even if it does not always show – there is no evidence that social drinking has any influence on cognitive function. To test this theory, extensive research has been done on twins over their lifetimes, and has shown that a modest regular intake of alcohol does not depress intellectual capacity, but on the contrary enhances it. Even better news from this research, conducted by a team from the Indiana University School of Medicine, is that this improvement in intellectual performance is unrelated to the type of drink; it applied equally whether the twins drank beer, wine or spirits.

"I'M CELEBRATING OUR EIGHTIETH"

The early signs of intellectual impairment caused by heavy and regular alcohol consumption can include such ill-defined symptoms as faulty judgement, loss of memory, difficulty in finding the right word and increased irritability, together with other personality changes and – most difficult of all to quantify – an impairment of abstract thinking. In a consistently heavy drinker there may be an inability or reluctance to think out problems for themselves, but rather to accept ready-made views, thereby losing their individuality of thought. This is sometimes obvious in elderly politicians who have been heavy tipplers for years. As time goes by, the opinions they express are all second-hand, derived from the Whip's office, delivered with great aplomb, but no more than a series of catch-phrases. The same problem can affect professional people: as long as the question they are asked is one they deal with regularly and they know the answer by heart, all is well. If confronted by a fresh situation, however, their intellectual impairment becomes obvious. These changes in cognitive function are often accompanied by a general lack of flexibility of thought, which can result in agitation if they are asked to perform a task which is different and at all complex.

These first signs of alcoholic dementia – the rather frightening term which describes the intellectual deterioration following heavy drinking – are often well-disguised. Minor changes in the memory, the judgement and the ease with which the subject becomes agitated may occur so slowly that they may not even be apparent to those who are living with the drinker.

Ironically, when the drinking is excessive the family may rally round and hide the problem from the outside world, which can simply cause added difficulties for all concerned. In Marie-Louise Meyer's *Drinking Problems* = *Family Problems,* she suggests that a partner who covers up for an alcoholic prevents him or her from becoming responsible for their own actions. The social and professional problems which can stem from the inevitable lies manufactured to protect the drinker can destroy the whole family.

Alcoholic dementia is associated with cerebral atrophy, or shrinkage of the brain, which can be readily demonstrated by an MRI scan. A survey done in San Francisco showed that this atrophy is not always persistent and that once the drinker has given up the scan may return to normal. The study showed that although some intellectual impairment could still be detected, the architecture of the brain was in most cases no different to that of the control group. This is particularly encouraging news for younger heavy drinkers who are able to stop their habit, for in this age group the intellectual deficit, as well as the anatomical changes, seem to be reversible.

The two conditions classically associated with the dementias caused by alcoholism are Korsakoff's syndrome and Wernicke's encephalopathy.

Korsakoff's syndrome is a chronic condition caused by long-term heavy drinking. It traditionally has three aspects: memory loss, confabulation (the making up of stories to compensate for the lack of memory) and peripheral neuropathy (loss of sensation in the limbs). Other psychiatric problems may be added to this trio of symptoms. In many cases the disorder has been preceded by episodes of delirium tremens, which happens from time to time in people who have been drinking for several years and have then suddenly stopped for a period.

The syndrome is the result of a deficiency of thiamine and possibly other members of the vitamin B group. Tragically, although treatment with vitamin B may stop the decline, some of the symptoms are irreversible; it is unusual for the patient to make a complete recovery.

Wernicke's encephalopathy is an altogether more sinister condition. It too is the result of deficiency of the vitamin B complex, but in this case the deficiency produces acute symptoms related to haemorrhage within the brain, like a large number of minute strokes. The patient has an unsteady gait, slow speech, flickering eyes and often a squint. Immediate treatment is even more important than with Korsakoff's syndrome, for Wernicke's encephalopathy can prove fatal. Improvement follows the treatment, but some permanent damage can be expected, as it would be after any cerebral vascular disaster.

One very rare condition, Marchiafava-Bignami disease, causes brain damage that results in sudden loss of balance, a staggering walk, irresponsible and irrational behaviour and often eventual coma. It was thought that this unusual disease was limited to middle-aged men who drank too much rough red Italian wine. Marchiafava-Bignami is now diagnosed more readily through scanning, and it is now known that the old views on the condition were an unwarranted smear on Italian wines. People of either sex and any nationality may occasionally suffer from Marchiafava-Bignami if they drink too much. It never occurs in moderate drinkers and it is suggested that malnutrition may play a part in its aetiology.

If Korsakoff's syndrome and Wernicke's encephalopathy are known to every medical student, delirium tremens is the manifestation of heavy drinking that is portrayed on the stage and mocked in comedians' jokes. Contrary to popular belief, DTs is not just a term to describe the fine tremor that drinkers develop after a heavy session the night before; it is a confusional state in which the drinker is agitated and suffers delusions. Compared to the mental changes, the very marked tremor is unimportant. DTs is usually the result of a period of abstinence, or a reduction in drinking, in somebody who has been drinking to excess for many years. Binge drinking can induce an attack; this may not be prevented even if the subject drinks in moderation after his binge.

A few years ago a colleague of mine, sent to America to cover an election, thought that a few weeks away from the social life of

"I CAN'T FIND A THING WRONG WITH YOU"

London would be an admirable opportunity to go on the wagon. On her second night in the States she developed classic DTs: a coarse tremor of her limbs – and, rather more worrying, of her eyelids – together with palpitations, sweating, nightmares and hallucinations.

When depicted on stage, the hallucinations are always predominantly visual and tactile; the victim characteristically sees and feels snakes. In fact, auditory hallucinations predominate. In my friend's case her hallucinatory horror was rats: she felt and saw rats, but above all, and more frightening than anything, she *heard* them. Luckily, she had some suitable medication with her, and after a good sleep was able to return to London, mission unaccomplished, but with the determination to modify her drinking. Her determination lapsed and I am told that she still has vodka with her breakfast orange juice.

Every now and again the hallucinations of DTs drive a heavy drinker to violence. In one instance, a local hero, a winner of the VC in the trenches, was called upon to restrain a local notable whose attack of DTs had resulted in an orgy of destruction in a local street. The VC, who had braved bullets as he went 'over the top', decided that on this occasion discretion was the better part of valour, and took refuge in the safety of his own front room.

Treatment of DTs is by prescription of benzodiazepines such as valium – which will stop the patient from having a fit – coupled with rest in subdued, but not frighteningly isolated, surroundings. The anti-psychotic drugs used to control hallucinations in other patients are not recommended, as the hallucinations from DTs are only temporary and such drugs can in these cases have bad effects on the blood pressure.

Alcohol withdrawal, even without the hallucinations or occasional fits, can be frightening both for the victim and those in attendance. Sudden withdrawal can produce all the physical symptoms found in DTs, but fits are very much more common than DTs in heavy drinkers and occur more often than is supposed when a hard-drinking patient stops after a major binge.

The damage excessive alcohol consumption can cause is not

confined to the central nervous system – the brain and the spinal cord – but it can also affect the peripheral nerves (such as those that supply the limbs and skin) and is one of the causes of a peripheral neuropathy which is thought to be more the result of vitamin deficiency than the toxicity of the alcohol. This neuropathy is characterized by loss of power in the muscles, but is also associated with a loss of sensation. Patients with a peripheral neuropathy of the feet feel as if they are walking on cotton wool; they do not receive the normal sensations when their feet hit the pavement. Loss of cutaneous nerve sensibility is also thought to be a factor in the development of impotence in persistent heavy drinkers.

Peripheral neuropathy can be caused by sensitivity to a great many toxic agents, but may also be the result of a deficiency of the B vitamins. It is this nutritional deficiency which causes the polyneuropathy found in alcoholics. It is interesting to watch a man who has been a persistently heavy drinker for years walking down the road: the lack of sensation gives him an unsteady gait, and he lifts his feet high with each step in the hope that by banging them down he will be able to elicit some sensory response. This is technically known as the 'hackney gait': the man is lifting his legs as if he were a hackney horse in a trotting race.

Now that the anatomy of the brain is easily explored with the MRI scanner, we can see that its function, sensitive to the smallest changes, seems to be little altered by moderate drinking, improved by light drinking and damaged only by heavy drinking. Some of these changes seem to be more related to the indirect effects of heavy drinking, such as the vitamin deficiencies, but there is also intellectual blunting and impairment of cognitive function, even in those who maintain a good diet but drink to excess.

11

Alcohol and old age

A patient consulted me recently about his father, who had become a heavy drinker in his eighties. The father, a very successful and charming man, was a widower who had grown tired of retirement, solitude and probably of life. My initial thought had been that he was depressed, which can be difficult to diagnose in the elderly as they tend to have less clearly defined symptoms than younger sufferers. However, after many long and honest consultations, it was obvious that he was not depressed, merely fed up. He could not understand his family's anxiety over his drinking. He explained that he never got drunk, did not create any problems and that he enjoyed the alcohol. He had always been a wine lover, and if his intake had now gone up from half a bottle to a bottle a night, did it really matter? I was forced to agree with him that it did not.

There is one aspect of ageism that manages to be 'politically correct'. Many younger people who pride themselves on encouraging the elderly to lead a full life and who would hate to think of themselves as being patronizing, are prejudiced against drinking among the older age groups. No sooner has an octogenarian picked up a glass than some busybody rushes to take it away from them with 'Not at your time of life, Dad.' How wrong those around them can be!

So good is the effect of alcohol in old age that it is now recommended in many old people's homes. This is a rediscovery of a previously accepted clinical truth. In my father's day, he would recommend as a tonic for the elderly, or sometimes for other age groups too, a glass of Guinness in the mornings for the poorer patients and a glass of dry sherry or champagne for those who had greater funds.

Research, much of it carried out in the United States – which does not usually look kindly on the medicinal qualities of alcohol – has shown that modest drinking helps older patients. In one experiment, elderly in-patients with Alzheimer's disease or similar conditions were randomly divided into two groups. One half was given vodka and orange for their mid-morning drink, the other orange. They had had some sweets beforehand to blunt their taste-buds. Neither the nurses who handed out the drink nor, of course, the recipients knew if they were receiving the laced orange or not. The elderly, confused patients who had the vodka were more co-operative with the staff, less incontinent (which is surprising), and chatted more animatedly to their fellow residents. After a time the groups were reversed, at which those who had been co-operative and jolly became silent once more, and the other group enjoyed a happier life-style. Recent research carried out by Dr Jean Marc Orgogozo among 3,777 people over the age of 65 confirmed that the onset of Alzheimer's is delayed in 75 per cent of those patients who have been accustomed to moderate drinking.

A paper published in the *American Journal of Medicine* and researched by Anne Volper, then supervisor of nursing at Cushing Hospital in Framingham, Massachusetts, and Professor Robert Kastenbaum, then director of psychological research at the hospital, discussed the use of beer, amongst other measures, to improve the environment of a ward devoted to the care of psychogeriatric elderly men. The ward's new regime included, as well as the beer, the provision of a record player, cards, adequate table space for eating as well as a smart shirt and tie every day. The long-term aim was to restore the patients' morale, thereby increasing their ability to fit better into society, even if that society was only hospital-based.

The experiment was a great success. Within a month the atmosphere of the ward in general, and the behaviour of the individual patients in particular, had improved. The amount of medication the patients needed was reduced, as was the number requiring medication. Within two months none of the patients were taking

Largactil (chlorpromazine), a powerful anti-psychotic drug used to tranquillize the agitated and irrational, whereas when the experiment started 75 per cent of those in the ward had been taking it daily. Most of the patients had previously been incontinent and some had needed physical restraint, but once they were treated in a more companionable way – and, despite the beer, had regained control of their bladders – most were no longer disruptive. Instead of sitting in rows, uncommunicative and unsmiling, they were wandering around the ward and chatting to each other and the staff. They made small purchases for themselves outside the hospital, and became so well socialized that they started to buy presents for others.

Although it was felt that each one of the various improvements had played its part in the restoration of the patients' morale, the provision of slightly more than half a pint of beer a day seems to have been the pivotal element. The beer was immediately recognized by the patients when it was first served, and was greeted with great enthusiasm. Subsequently, if it was ever withheld – as it was on occasions to test the reaction of the patients – its lateness in arriving was immediately noted.

The psychologist decided that the value of the beer – wine apparently worked equally well – lay in the fact that drinking has a symbolic significance. Having a drink made the old men who had been parcelled away from mainstream life feel that, once again, they were people in their own right. Just as in late adolescence beer had been the indicator that they were adult, so in old age and in the hospital ward, the opportunity to drink convinced them that they could still look after themselves and make their own informed decisions, such as going to the lavatory and buying small items in the shops.

When discussing alcohol intake with older patients, however, the possibility that they are taking other medicines which might be incompatible with alcohol or might enhance its effects must be borne in mind. Nowhere is this more true than in long-stay hospitals.

A few years ago a study in California looked at a group of

patients of sixty-five or over who had had their health and life-style assessed in middle age. As one would expect, being poor was not a good prognostic sign for a healthy and happy retirement, nor was having a high blood pressure, being a heavy drinker or smoking. Encouragingly, however, those who had a moderate alcohol intake over the previous twenty years, and who were still drinking when older, were well over twice as likely to be active, happy and healthy than those who were abstainers.

Professor Robert Kastenbaum has become one of the leading experts in the United States on the care of the elderly, and in 1988 he published a review on the humane care of older people in hospital. His conclusions were:

> There is by now sufficient information available to indicate that moderate use of alcoholic beverages is pleasurable and beneficial for older adults . . . the lower ethanol beverages such as beer and wine may have their place in the lifestyles of some older adults.

The evidence for Professor Kastenbaum's conclusions came from many sources, including the major study by the American National Institute of Alcoholism and Alcohol Abuse. This showed that when one or two drinks were taken by older people each day, even when in a nursing or retirement home, they had better morale, were less likely to worry, slept better and were better socially orientated. Conversely, older people who refused their drinks were more likely to show regressive behaviour.

This large study also suggested that alcohol improves the physique as well as the social and behavioural performance. In summary, Professor Kastenbaum said that alcohol stimulated residents' power of thought and led to more effective use of their remaining mental, social and emotional attributes. The professor was particularly struck by the improvement in the reasoning powers of those who had had a drink, and said that from a scientific point of view this was the most interesting finding.

The Department of Medical and Molecular Genetics at Indiana

University studied the effect of alcohol on the intellectual power (cognitive function) in 4,739 sets of twins as they aged. The individuals were born between 1917 and 1927. Tests were designed to assess their intellectual capabilities, and the results were reassuring. Once again there was the J-shaped curve, the teetotallers and the heavy drinkers scoring worse than those who were moderate drinkers. Not only did the ageing twins fare better if they were still drinking, but there was a suggestion that even if they had now stopped drinking, their past moderate drinking had a small protective effect on their performance when older.

Apart from the obvious health risks of heavy drinking, there is also the danger of a fall and subsequent fracture. However, as we have seen, research does not support the oft-repeated warning that drinking moderately is a factor in osteoporosis: bone mineral density is in fact higher in social or moderate drinkers than in those who are either heavy drinkers or teetotallers.

Possibly in no age group is the social drink more important than in the septuagenarian and octogenarian. One of the tricks of

"GWEN AND I HAVE CALCULATED WE CAN LIVE FOREVER"

growing old gracefully is to remain part of society – a glass of wine enjoyed with the whole family, neighbours or former colleagues may do far more good than a whole packet of antidepressants. The stresses of life change with the passage of the years: the anxieties of youth and middle age are past, and as they went, so too goes the temptation to drink more than is 'wise'. Older people have a very reasonable fear of losing control: they feel vulnerable, both physically and mentally, and are therefore reluctant to jeopardize their stability and security.

Any anxious and elderly moderate drinker should be reassured by a 1994 research project in America which looked at the drinking patterns of many thousands of women over sixty-five. The report showed that they had better neuromuscular co-ordination – they were 'steadier on their pins' – than non-drinkers. This survey, together with an increasing number of similar studies from the United States, confirms earlier suggestions that those who are no more than moderate drinkers can expect a happier as well as longer life.

For most people, alcohol in moderation is more likely to improve rather than damage their health. Because alcohol is dangerous in excess, its advantages are often overlooked.

Set yourself a limit before you start an evening's drinking.

Try to keep track of when and what you drink.

Avoid drinking on an empty stomach.

It is better to drink at meal times, or at any rate with some food. Snacks should be served when drinks are offered.

Be aware of the difficulties of measuring a drink when pouring one at home. Most home-poured gins and whiskies are at least double the tot provided by the local publican (see table on p. 9).

Drink slowly, and dilute spirits with at least as much water. This might shock the Scots but it would help their health.

12

Alcohol and cancer

The very word 'cancer' strikes terror into the most urbane of people. It is not, however, a detailed diagnosis because there are many different types of malignancy and they have very different consequences. Cancers can vary from the rodent ulcer on the face, cured in a matter of moments, to cancer of the oesophagus, which has a depressingly high mortality.

Not only is the diagnosis of cancer terrifying, but such has been the desire to live a healthy life – encouraged by the propaganda of the 'back to nature' Green movement – that there is sometimes an assumption the disease may have been the result of an unwise life-style. 'Perhaps,' some sufferers might think, 'my cancer could have been avoided if I had lived in the Highlands rather than on Clapham Common, had never smoked, avoided meat, eaten wholemeal rather than white bread, eschewed foods produced with artificial fertilizers and, above all, refused to drink alcohol.'

As a research team from the University of Louisville reported in the journal of *Cancer Education* in 1993, the evidence to support a 'cause and effect' relationship between alcohol and cancers was far from unanimous. The Louisville team came to its conclusion despite the categorical statement of the World Health Organisation (WHO) that 'alcoholic beverages are carcinogenic to humans'.

The WHO statement needs to be analysed carefully, as it may have been influenced by international politics and religious belief. *The Journal of Cancer Education*, commenting on the statement, said that 'the scientific literature extant in 1992 provides only fairly weak support for that finding'. Yet despite its critical reception by detached authorities, the WHO opinion is frequently quoted by opponents of alcohol.

As with every other aspect of the subject, the association between alcohol and cancer essentially concerns excessive rather than moderate drinking, and its effect is greatly enhanced by simultaneous smoking.

One of the earliest associations between alcohol and cancer learned by every third-year medical student is that between cancer of the oesophagus (gullet) and spirit drinking. As medical students in the 1950s we were taught (and, when qualified, taught) that Calvados drinkers in Normandy, like whisky drinkers in areas of Scotland where there were distilleries, had a particularly high incidence of cancer of the oesophagus. Recent analysis has shown that there is indeed a risk of incurring the disease from the spirits in question, but that it does not affect light or moderate drinkers. People who smoke as well as drink are very much more likely to develop cancer of the oesophagus. It is possible that other factors as well as tobacco may act synergistically with alcohol to initiate these tumours. The survey also shows that the relationship between alcohol and cancer of the oesophagus is only relevant in those drinkers whose intake exceeded the safe dose recommended by the government by a factor of three or four.

Furthermore, the news that will hearten every whisky drinker is that whisky taken in very modest amounts, about two units a day, actually lowers the incidence of cancer of the oesophagus. Although the link between whisky drinkers and rats is tenuous, it is interesting that experiments conducted with rats trained to drink whisky to the tune of the equivalent of one bottle a day have not produced the changes in their cells that would be expected to foretell malignancy.

Of the 441 articles published by 1992 in the medical press about the links between drinking on cancer, only 29 were judged to meet the requirements of even an acceptable meta-analysis. There is , for example, nothing in the literature about alcohol and cancer that comes near to paralleling the research findings that linked cigarette smoking with cancer. Despite this paucity of evidence, it is required by law in California – a health-conscious and otherwise sophisticated state – to display in those places where alcohol is on sale a notice to this effect:

Warning: Drinking distilled spirits, beers, coolers and other alcoholic beverages may increase cancer risk and during pregnancy cause birth defects.

Smokers, as well as facing an increased chance of developing cancer of the oesophagus, also have to acknowledge that there is a proven relationship between heavy drinking and cancer of the nasal spaces, salivary glands, larynx and mouth. Cancer is usually multi-factorial and family history is of relevance, but the synergistic action of tobacco with alcohol is a risk that cannot be ignored by heavy drinkers.

This risk is not one which should disturb the social drinker who enjoys his two to four glasses of wine a day. An oft-repeated suggestion is that the dark spirits – whisky, Calvados, brandy and many liqueurs – contain more cancer-promoting agents than the light ones such as vodka, gin, white rum and tequila It is also suggested that the congeners, the non-alcoholic constituents of various drinks, may be carcinogenic. Research workers from the National Cancer Institute in Bethesda have investigated this theory and have found no scientific evidence to support it. Congeners may cause immediate problems – a hang-over – but there is no evidence that they will give rise to cancers.

The American figures showing that 75 per cent of oesophageal cancers and 50 per cent of oral cavity cancers are associated with drinking have to be viewed in the light of the fact that no experimental studies have shown that alcohol by itself is carcinogenic in these areas. The assumption made to reconcile these two pieces of research is that alcohol is a tumour promoter which needs some other factor to act synergistically with it before a cancer can develop. The suggestion is that tobacco is the most common of these synergistic factors, and that malnourishment, which often accompanies alcoholism, is another. In general, my advice to patients is always that if they drink in moderation they should not suffer any additional risk of developing cancer, but that even if they drink in moderation they should not combine this with smoking.

A contemporary of mine, George, whom I had known since university days, was very hard-drinking, though he never appeared drunk. He worked in the media at a time when lunch was still a boozy affair. It would be an unusual day when he did not have a couple of double gin and tonics before lunch, a bottle of wine with the meal and repeat the same pattern in the evening, probably with a few glasses of brandy after dinner. As a younger man George was not one to embrace his vices singly: he also smoked a hundred cigarettes a day. One day George noticed that he had a red, ulcerating spot at the back of his mouth behind his molars. He went to see his dentist on a few occasions, but he did not seem very interested, and so George came to his doctor instead.

The large spot, by now bleeding, looked appallingly malignant – although in these cases looks can be misleading. Unfortunately, in George's case they were not. He has had extensive treatment and seems to be doing well, although the radiotherapy has given him an unpleasantly dry mouth. There is evidence that if patients who have had the cancer treated continue to smoke and drink heavily they have a greatly increased chance of a recurrence or the development of a second primary cancer.

The evidence linking cancer of the stomach with alcohol is less convincing than that linking heavy drinking and smoking with nasal/oral and oesophageal tumours. Although alcohol's main effect as a carcinogen is on the upper digestive tract, there is also evidence of an increased incidence of potentially malignant polyps in the large bowel and of cancer of the rectum. Research by the University of Texas has confirmed the association between alcohol and pre-malignant adenomatous polyps, but suggests that the true association is with cigarette smoking, or cigarette smoking and heavy drinking, rather than with alcohol on its own. There is no doubt that cigarette smoking combined with heavy alcohol consumption increases the risk of polyps, and that this is more apparent if the patient is still smoking rather than if he or she smoked in the past.

Evidence for the relationship between drinking – when not combined with smoking – and cancer of the colon and rectum is uncertain, even contradictory. Some research has suggested that alcohol intake is more likely to affect the rectum rather than the colon, whereas other surveys have found the converse to be true: drinkers are more likely to suffer from cancer of the transverse and descending colon, but cancers of the first part of the colon, the ascending colon, and the rectum bear no relation to the patient's drinking habits.

It has also been suggested that the link between malignancies of the large gut and alcohol can be influenced by the type of drink taken. A 1993 study suggested that reports claiming beer drinkers had an increased liability to colo-rectal cancer were over-simplifications, and that such links as there were applied mainly to the rectum. There is some good news for wine drinkers: a study published in 1994 reported that wine appeared to provide some protection from cancer to the last part of the colon. This research also found no increase in cancer of the first part of the colon or rectum that could be associated with drinking.

The association between cancer of the liver and alcohol is an indirect one, and is dealt with in Chapter 8.

Few topics have been more fiercely debated than the influence of alcohol on cancer of the breast. The evidence is even more contradictory than that relating to colo-rectal cancer. One study published in *The British Journal of Cancer* in 1994 even came to the remarkable conclusion that women who were moderate drinkers were less likely to suffer cancer of the breast. The general medical view is that drinkers seem to have a fractionally increased risk of developing the condition, but the causal link has not been established; if there is an association, it is a very weak one.

The difficulty research workers have is in separating the effect of alcohol consumption from all the other factors that may affect the development of this particular tumour. Weight, social background and diet may all have a part to play. It is supposed that all these determinants increase oestrogen levels, which are known to affect the chances of developing a breast tumour. One highly regarded team of research workers has even suggested that there may be a tenuous relationship between high levels of the cardio-protective blood fat HDL and cancer of the breast.

Reassuringly, the very large population studies have shown that not only do women who drink in moderation have a lower all-cause mortality, mainly because of their reduced liability to heart attacks, but that this advantage is still apparent even when allowance has been made for the lower death rate from cardiac disease.

Although there may be doubt about the significance of drinking to cancer of the breast in women, it is of prime importance when the tumour grows in men. I was telephoned by a friend and patient who had noticed one hot summer's afternoon, when the jackets were off, that his colleague's shirt was bloodstained where it covered his left breast. The colleague came straight round in a taxi, and on examination I found that he had a hard tumour about the size of a horse chestnut. The patient's history is a classic one: there is a background of cancer of the breast in the family and he drinks heavily. He is not the type of man who would be bothered if his alcohol intake exceeded the recommended four units a day and twenty-eight in a week: his consumption has probably not been less than one hundred units a week for years. The connection between drinking and cancer of the breast in men is firmly established, and is easily explained by the assumption that alcohol reduces the testosterone and increases the oestrogen.

Just as these hormonal changes would be expected to make cancer of the breast more likely in men, so might they be expected to reduce the incidence of cancer and benign enlargement of the prostate. Cancer of the prostate is certainly testosterone-dependent, and it is likely that the benign enlargement is also hormonally governed. Research-based evidence for this is lacking, but there has recently been a report from the Far East which noted a reduction in the incidence in older men of obstructive uropathy resulting from enlargement of the prostate. For men who drank at least 25 ounces of alcohol a month, whether in beer, wine or saké, the risk was almost halved. Other spirits had no influence either way.

One curious effect of alcohol in relation to cancer is the symptom described by Dr Jan de Winter and now known as de Winter's symptom. When Dr de Winter was working at the Royal Marsden Hospital in London nearly forty years ago, he noticed that patients with Hodgkin's disease (a lymphoma) sometimes developed severe backache after drinking before they had any other indication of the disease. There are, however, many other causes of backache when drinking, ranging from an osteoarthritic back stressed by having to stand for too long to the pain from a thoroughly upset colon, which can radiate through to the back.

A letter to the *British Journal of Cancer* in 1993 suggested that moderate consumption of alcohol may protect against rather than cause some forms of cancer. The international panel of epidemiologists, toxicologists and pharmacologists who wrote the report had examined published data on cancers associated with the mouth and gastro-intestinal tract. They noticed that some of this material had not taken into account the effects of different levels of drinking. When the data was examined with varying intakes in mind, the panel revised its view. This re-examination showed that men who took two drinks of alcohol per day run half the risk of developing those cancers that abstainers do, whilst those drinking two to four drinks a day reduced this risk by two-thirds. Only men drinking twelve or more drinks (or units) a day had a greater risk than teetotallers.

It seems that where the oral and pharyngeal cancers are concerned, any likelihood of malignant change is enhanced by other factors, particularly smoking and possibly life-style differences such as malnourishment.

There is just a chance – no more than that at this stage of research – that one constituent of red wines, the flavonoid quercetin, may actually be active against cancer. Quercetin is found in abundance in red grapes when they have ripened under hot sun. It is also found in many other fruits, and in garlic and onions. Animal studies have shown that quercetin is effective in inhibiting cancer of the colon in mice; rutin, another flavonoid, has similar properties. It is not always meaningful to apply the scientific data collected from animals to humans, but there is some evidence that onion and garlic-eating communities suffer less malignant disease than those who eschew them.

An association has been suggested between the combination of smoking with heavy drinking and cancer of the bladder. There is certainly a relationship between smoking and this cancer, but evidence that drinking makes the relationship stronger is not convincing.

This chapter on alcohol intake and cancer has emphasized the message that drink taken in moderation does not seem to be pernicious, but that there is a link between heavy alcohol consumption and several cancers, particularly those of the oral cavity, the throat and the oesophagus, and possibly the colo-rectum. In each of these cancers, however, there are also likely to be other factors influencing the patient's liability to developing a tumour.

Empty your glass before you allow it to be refilled.

Avoid drinking at both lunchtime and in the evening.

Flavonoids are more abundant in red wine and dark beers than in other drinks. It is this abundance which gives these drinks an advantage, but other drinks also have a health-giving value.

Not all wines, even if the same colour, have equal cardioprotective qualities; flavonoid content depends on the type of grape, the nature of the soil, climate and the way in which the wine is made.

13

Alcoholics and heavy drinkers

Although categorizing heavy drinkers according to their drinking patterns and past history is now thought to be too simplistic – and even counterproductive – discussion with patients about their drinking habits reveals that there are broad groups into which they fit. These groups are not definitive, and some people's drinking may show characteristics of more than one category, but this unfashionable exercise does help in assessing their likely future behaviour.

When I was a junior doctor in psychiatry we had no compunction about labelling our patients according to their drinking practices. There were the social drinkers: these were likely to drink moderately, and we now know that their health would – unless they suffered one of the comparatively rare contra-indications to alcohol – be improved rather than harmed by it.

Although moderate social drinking, particularly of red wine, is now acknowledged as being healthy, there are still some prejudiced people who frown upon it. Those who are intolerant of drinkers become particularly agitated if someone makes a ritual of it. They regard with deepest suspicion the person whose drinking forms a daily pattern; without taking into consideration the amount drunk, they detect a potential dependency. Many workers in the field of alcoholism, whatever their role, therefore disapprove of those who routinely have a drink when they return from work – especially if they admit it is to help them relax after the stresses of the office rather than to enjoy a companionable half-hour with their partners. Although it is easy to condemn these domestic rituals and to see in them the start of an addictive pattern, they can be an important part of family life. This is not only because of the pharmacological effect of the alcohol, but also

"I'M HOME DARLING"

because the evening drink creates an opportunity for the household to come together at the end of the working day.

Social drinkers are apt to have half a bottle of wine or thereabouts with their meals. Like anyone else, they make take rather too much on celebratory occasions, but even if they are unfit to drive it is most unlikely that they will regularly be 'drunk'. Our forefathers would have described their condition after a good party as being 'a bit merry' or 'rather tight'.

There is another group of drinkers whose consumption of alcohol is excessive, though without it being a problem either to the family or to society at large. These used to be known as the 'heavy social drinkers'. They were to be seen enjoying a good lunch in the City, having a few drinks before returning home, a few more with their partners when they arrived, and finally a bottle of wine at dinner. Heavy social drinkers drank too much at parties and, unlike the ordinary social drinker, it was obvious to those around them that they were intoxicated. However, they were not 'blind drunk' and in general their behaviour was unlikely to be offensive.

Marie-Louise Meyer's book *Drinking Problems = Family Problems* is based on her experiences during many years of nursing and later as Director of the London Council on Alcoholism. Ms Meyer writes very tellingly of the characteristics of the heavy social drinker that distinguished them from the early stages of problem drinking.

The drinking pattern of the heavy social drinker was fixed, and there was no obvious progression towards heavier consumption. Indeed, in many cases as they grew older they drank less and became ordinary social drinkers who would not disgrace even the Vicar's annual sherry party. William was just such a man. He had a good war record, but had spent seven years in the army during the time that other generations would have been learning a profession. After the army William drifted from one venture to the next; the only thing each one had in common was that they all lost huge sums of money. As William's income decreased, his drinking increased, although he never became a solitary drinker. He had rather too much to drink with his lunch and rather too much when he first came home. At dinner he had more than his share of the bottle of wine, and always needed a few glasses of whisky while he decried the changing world as displayed on the *Ten O'Clock News*.

William, like other social drinkers, never lost control over the amount that he drank, and if circumstances demanded it, he could do without the alcohol. Heavy social drinkers would abstain if their work, driving or health made it necessary, which is what happened to William. Once he reached retirement age he started to drink less; the tension had gone out of his life, for he no longer had to see himself as a failure. One day his doctor told him that he had a dangerously high blood pressure; he must take the prescribed tablets and cut back on drinking. Thereafter William gave up alcohol almost entirely, although as a good host he now has one glass of wine at his own dinner parties.

Some heavy social drinkers have to pay a price for their pleasures, but part of the definition of this group is that they do not drink to the point where their habit damages their health, domestic and social life, or professional competence. They are always aware that, if their professional or domestic circumstances changed for the worse, they might be tempted to drown their sorrows by drinking more, and so drift into becoming a problem drinker. Most have the strength of will not to combat adversity with drink.

Drinking that may create mayhem and domestic discord in one environment – an overcrowded flat, perhaps – would hardly provoke comment in a rural castle. Likewise, convivial drinking is expected in some occupations but results in immediate dismissal in others. As the concept of how much drinking constitutes a problem varies from country to country, class to class and job to job, so does the definition of what is a problem drinker. Certainly, the amount of alcohol drunk is not the yardstick. I have always considered that my patients were problem drinkers once their habit damaged their family or professional lives, or when it created financial problems. Naturally, if for some reason their drinking was detrimental to their health, and yet they continued with it, this too could be described as problem drinking, even though the amount involved might have been small; the quantity that endangers health varies so much from person to person.

Those patients who drift from heavy social drinking to problem drinking may rely emotionally on alcohol, even if they are not technically addicted to it. To some of them, alcohol is the lifebelt which helps them to stay afloat in a turbulent world, whether the turbulence is brought on by a job which is too demanding (or not demanding enough) or by the storms of marital life. Sometimes the heavy social drinker becomes a problem drinker as a result of bereavement.

The recurring plea from anxious members of the heavy drinker's family is how to arrest the decline. In some cases, even if the person concerned is neither a problem drinker nor addicted, a period of abstinence is an easy way to reverse the

" IT'S JUST A SIP TO STEADY THE NERVES "

slide from heavy social drinker to problem drinker to alcoholic. In most cases, though, as the drinker is not addicted but at most psychologically dependent, it is possible to change subtly the environment so that the pretext for drinking is not there.

The acronym HALT ('hungry, angry, lonely or tired') should never be forgotten. The returning worker, tired and weary, must be given quick succour. He or she will be too overwrought to sit down immediately to steak and chips, for there is nothing more off-putting to a tense wage-slave than to be herded into the family dining-room the moment they are home. Many homecoming workers gain triple benefit from the pre-prandial drink: it eases the tension, relieves the hypoglycaemia (so long as dinner is not too long delayed) and enables them to settle back comfortably within their home environment.

The word 'alcoholic' is bandied about casually these days. It is an epithet far too loosely applied, and without due regard to its implications. Its misuse is not confined to lay chatter in bars or at parties; the modern, politically correct social worker is apt to describe problem drinkers, and even some heavy social drinkers, by the pejorative term 'alcoholic'. In medical practices today, unsubtle and vaguely critical questionnaires are issued to new patients and, if interpreted strictly, would suggest that many of the people attending with widely disparate symptoms really needed treatment for their drinking, although it has created no problems nor shows any sign of damaging their health. Unfortunately, similar questionnaires are also used in some psychiatric units; this can skew the diagnosis and therefore the treatment the patient receives.

Although everybody has a good idea of who is an alcoholic, the accurate description of 'alcoholism' is difficult. Since any attempt is subjective, and is bound to be coloured by personal or group prejudices, it is probably unhelpful to try to define the condition, but the World Health Organisation (WHO) has nevertheless attempted to do so. The result of its deliberations is unhelpfully vague: WHO describes alcoholics as excessive drinkers whose dependence on alcohol is noticeably interfering with their mental and physical health, with their family relationships and with their financial state.

The American Medical Association sees alcoholism as an illness:

> ... characterized by a significant impairment, which is directly associated with persistent and excessive use of alcohol. Impairment may involve physiological, psychological or social dysfunction.

Perhaps it is more useful to follow the thoughts of E. M. Jellinek, whose research into alcoholism is the basis of much of present-day thinking. In 1960 Jellinek suggested that there are five different types of alcoholic, which he labelled from Alpha to Epsilon.

In Alpha alcoholism there is psychological but not physiological dependence. Alpha alcoholics rely upon the tranquillizing effect of alcohol to ease them through the social difficulties of life;

some may drink in order to forget, even for a short while, the traumas of the day. These people's drinking habits are the result of trying to cope with life's problems in the way most readily available to them.

Jellinek's Beta alcoholics belong to the same general type as Alpha, but in their case the drinking has resulted in impairment of some of their bodily systems. They may be suffering from liver disease, chronic gastritis or have a peripheral neuropathy. They are the problem drinkers who are beginning to pay for their habit with ill-health.

In vino veritas applies to all drinkers, but in none is it better illustrated than in the resentful, tense person. Their anxieties and prejudices remain hidden as long as they have not been drinking, but after sometimes only two or three drinks the underlying aggression is exposed. This is particularly well demonstrated by the Gamma type.

Gamma alcoholics would be recognized for what they are by even the least observant layman. They are physically as well as psychologically addicted to alcohol; they display a marked degree of tolerance to its effects and therefore consume large amounts. Invariably, their health will be suffering and their behaviour, both in and out of their homes, is anti-social.

Some Gamma alcoholics manage to cope well with life, but this is usually because they are solitary people with adequate financial support who do not have to interrelate with other people or earn a living. A good example of a Gamma alcoholic well adapted to his own life-style was a retired City solicitor whose wife had died some years previously. The patient, who was in his early eighties, lived by himself and his house was kept clean by others. Unfortunately, after his wife died his heavy social drinking – he had been a great host in his time – progressed to alcoholic dependency. He started by drinking Madeira with his morning coffee, a quaint Edwardian custom, and finished late at night, bemused and slightly unsteady, on brandy. His behaviour outraged his family, who constantly argued for his admission to a psychiatric unit for treatment. Since he was happy and safe, since he ate well and his physical health did not seem to be deteriorating as fast as that of other octogenarians, it was hard to see what advantage enforced teetotalism was going to provide to his last years in this world.

Although this retired solicitor was unusual in that his drinking did not strain his financial resources and he had a very reasonable home environment, most drinkers of this type will not live in such comfort. The elderly 'regular' in the local pub who shuffles across the street each morning to lay claim to his favourite chair may well be an alcoholic who has remained well-integrated with his local society. This type is often popular, an accepted 'character' of the district who is welcomed by the landlord as well as the other customers. Contrary to popular belief, alcoholism does not always change someone's personality, but its disinhibitory effect reveals their true character by taking the wrappers off the character they like to display to the world.

However, most Gamma alcoholics are the hard-drinking, addicted drunks who are a nuisance in social and professional life, who almost invariably lose their jobs and their families and often end up in the courts. This type of drinking is considered essentially Anglo-Saxon. A good example is Richard; he was born into privileged surroundings, just too late even to have had to go into the army for compulsory military service. He has never worked, but has always drunk to excess; there has never been any balance between work and play. By his late teens he was a problem drinker, and by the time he married he was a Gamma alcoholic. Despite his love for his children, the marriage could not stand the strain. Now, lonely, impoverished and with severe liver disease, he faces an inevitably early end.

The Delta alcoholics are reputed to be found more often in wine-drinking countries. They always have a glass in their hand; they can be seen sitting in French cafés at breakfast time drinking brandy. They appear never to be sober, and they keep up their drinking all day long. Delta alcoholics are also known as 'inveterate drinkers'. In this country their counterparts are not to be seen sitting at café tables, but lying in doorways.

"I FIND THE SOBER-UP PILL IS BEST TAKEN WITH A QUADRUPLE WHISKY"

The Epsilon alcoholics are a fascinating study. They are the really serious binge drinkers. After days, weeks or months of total sobriety, they will have a drinking spree of variable length; it may be just for a day or two, but could last for a week or longer.

Some Gamma alcoholics become Epsilon alcoholics as they grow older. Age has taught them some caution, but not enough. One sixty-five-year-old man had drifted from social drinking to problem drinking before he was persuaded to stop. Outwardly he became a model citizen, but occasional early morning telephone calls from police stations around the country kept me aware of the true state of affairs. Sobriety was too difficult for this particular patient, and every few months he would go on a 'bender' in some distant town. He finally died, sober.

Many people drift into alcoholism, having graduated from heavy social drinking to problem drinking. This downward slide is often not initially noticed by others in the family. When they start to drink heavily, many men do so away from home. They drink with their colleagues from work, have a few drinks on the way home or in their clubs, and become adept at hiding their habit.

After the death of one MP, his widow became president of the local Conservative Association, taking her duties very seriously. Month after month she entertained the women's advisory committees to tea; the sandwiches were beautifully cut and Lady Smith's only idiosyncrasy was that she liked to have her tea poured from a small silver pot – which she claimed had great sentimental value – before adding some milk. One day, a highly suspicious party worker managed to swap the contents of the teapots and, as she suspected, found it was not sentiment but whisky which made Lady Smith reluctant to have her tea from the communal urn. The good lady continued to conduct her meetings with great aplomb, and such was the regard in which she was held that thereafter she was able to drink a whisky – without the milk and from a glass – while the others had their tea. In Lady Smith's case, her wealth and her ability not to drink to the point of becoming intoxicated preserved her from undesirable financial or social consequences. Had she had a different background, her behaviour might have been considered reprehensible rather than merely 'eccentric'.

Not all spouses want to recognize their partner's gradual decline into heavy drinking, and if they do notice the signs, their approach to the problem will vary enormously. The attitude of wives – there are five times more male alcoholics than female – to heavy drinking is to some extent determined by their own upbringing, their age and their relationship with their husband. Being brought up as a child in a heavy-drinking household can have very varied effects on people when they are older.

Some are so put off by their early experiences of domestic discord that they are absurdly strict with their husbands and may become worried beyond reason by his third gin and tonic. They feel certain that this minor lapse is a sign that the next stage in the Rake's Progress will be destitution and admission to a clinic. Others, remembering the terminal alcoholism of a parent, may dismiss problem drinking as being nothing compared to the signs and symptoms displayed by their father, and thereby lose an opportunity of halting their partner's lapse into chronic alcoholism. No alcoholic suffers alone; even the drunk in the street doorway has close relatives who mourn his absence even as they blame themselves, feeling that if only they had acted differently this disaster would not have befallen their child, sibling, partner or parent. Alcoholism has such a complex and multifactorial aetiology that apportioning blame is pointless – but it is easier to prevent than to cure.

A recurrent question from the relatives of people who might

broadly be classified as alcoholics is whether the condition is hereditary. This topic generates a remarkable amount of ill-feeling as it raises passionate sentiments. Many sufferers from alcoholism are convinced that it is a specific disease, probably associated with abnormalities in the structure or functioning of the higher centres of the brain. If this is so, it must inevitably have an hereditary aspect. Others feel that it is not the alcoholism which is inherited, but a personality type which may lead people to rely heavily on alcohol to help them through life's battles. It is this latter point of view which generates the most resentment and anger.

Whatever the cause, there is no doubt that the child of an alcoholic is four times more likely to become alcoholic than somebody born to a moderate drinker. Some of this may well be a result of the environment, but this explanation is not entirely supported by twin and adoption studies, for even when the child of an alcoholic has been raised in an abstemious home, research shows they are more likely to become problem drinkers. It is unlikely that any one gene is responsible. The inheritance of alcoholism is probably the result of a combination of genes whose effect on the personality can be influenced by the nature of the upbringing.

An Outline of Psychiatry by Clarence J. Rowe and Walter D. Mink quotes evidence which suggests, strangely, that the children of very puritanical, teetotal homes are more likely to become alcoholics than those brought up amongst moderate drinkers. Extreme views on alcohol, like extreme views on most subjects, can cause rebellion as well as acquiescence.

The argument over the hereditary nature, or otherwise, of alcoholism is one that is familiar throughout medicine and can be summed up as 'nature versus nurture'. Both factors are of importance, but to varying degrees in different people.

A convincing (but recently disputed) case can be made out for there being two different patterns of alcohol dependence, one seeming to have a stronger hereditary pattern than the other. Men who start drinking in their teenage years and become dependent very quickly often have fathers who drank to excess. In these people the abnormal drinking is frequently associated with aberrant personality traits such as violence, impulsive behaviour or other addictive habits. Once these early heavy drinkers have become abstemious, they are rarely, if ever, able to resume moderate drinking. There is a strong hereditary link in this type of early-onset alcoholism.

The other type of alcoholic progresses from heavy drinking to problem drinking and then to alcoholism. In these people, nurture seems more likely than nature to have determined their style of drinking, so that by the time they are alcoholics they are usually well beyond teenage years. After a period of abstinence, many of these patients – the late-onset alcoholics who have no strong family history of the condition – are able to return to socialized light drinking.

Any discussion on alcoholism has to take into account the fact that only a small proportion of people will ever drink so much as to be classified as alcoholic. The Americans suggest that one in thirteen in the USA have a problem as a result of drinking, although 80 to 90 per cent of the population drinks alcohol. In many cases the problems of temperament that have led to alcohol addiction would have manifested themselves in some other form if alcohol had not been available. Alcoholism is not just the result of a weak person being unable to resist temptation, and heavy drinking is not confined to any one personality type – it includes people with every sort of psychopathology.

It is very often difficult to determine whether the symptoms of which the patient complains are those of alcoholism, or of the condition which has led to the drinking. One banker who had had a very satisfactory career came to see me because he was drinking more and more. He was never drunk, but now he liked to have a couple of drinks before his lunch if he could manage it, and he was apt to take rather more wine to keep the bank's guests company at lunchtime than his colleagues thought was necessary. In the evenings he usually persuaded his wife that it would be a good idea to open a second bottle, as 'we can always leave anything over for tomorrow'. There never was anything left in the bottle the following day.

This banker was quite certain that he was not depressed. Many lay people – my patient amongst them – believe that depression is a sign of inadequacy, that depressives are feeble people who break down and sob into their pillows at night. However, many cases of affective disorder, the depressive psychosis, affect people whose past record is one of success, socially as well as professionally. Only when they become depressed does their work performance fall away – or if it does not fall away, it can only be maintained for a time by huge endeavour. The banker, exhausted by the strain of competing when he was feeling so lacklustre, was only able to survive with the help of alcohol. I told him that his primary problem was not alcoholism but his depressive nature; he did not believe me, but within three weeks of starting his anti-depressant tablets he was back on top form. No one had mentioned his heavy drinking after the first interview, but once his mood had returned to normal he told me that his compulsion to drink had totally vanished.

Surveys of former alcoholics carried out by psychiatrists who did not know their subjects' previous history revealed an abnormally high incidence of other psychiatric troubles, even when allowance was made for the psychological consequences of the earlier alcoholism. Not all psychiatric problems are as easily resolved as those of my depressed banker, however. Many need very long-term treatment, and in some of them alcohol is contra-indicated as it tends to make control of the disease more difficult.

In other cases the heavy drinking may be part of a personality disorder. People with such disorders find it difficult, if not impossible, to establish what is thought of as 'normal' relationships with other people; their maladaptive personality has aspects which lead to a repetitive type of anti-social behaviour. These people have a low tolerance of stress, and if the world does not go their way, often drink heavily to relieve tensions. Patients with a personality disorder have the advantage that any mayhem their drinking causes will not usually bring lasting anxiety: their consciences are rather blunted as they tend to see the world only from their own point of view.

Whatever the causes of alcoholism, there is one safe bet: the drinker will deny it, initially to himself or herself as well as to others. In psychiatric terms they become defensive, but as strategists they do not display originality: they all present the same defence and the doctor usually sees straight through it.

In *The Outline of Psychiatry*, Rowe and Mink suggest that alcoholics adopt four basic pretexts: rationality, denial, projection and disassociation. These are easily understood and identifiable:

Rationality Finding dubious reasons to explain the necessity for drinking. We all know the sort of excuses they produce: it is essential to drink in order to bring in business, to strengthen commercial associations, or because it is part of the job. Just such a man is Henry. He is in sales, and he is very good at his job, one of the best: kindly but tough, generous but demanding. He is a wonderful host, and there are few days when he does not preside over a lunch; he follows this with champagne before dinner and wine with the meal. He never becomes bad-tempered, and if he feels irritable he is very adept at hiding it. Henry's excuse for drinking is that it is part of the formula which has made him a multi-millionaire.

Denial This is denial even to themselves. In its most bland form, this may be underestimating the amount drunk at a party or during an evening with friends, or the number of times that they have an evening drink with colleagues before going home. In extreme cases it is no longer a matter of exaggeration, but simply of lying. This is the person who says to his partner after the party that he has had only three glasses of wine, even though she and the other people present noticed that the heavy drinker's glass was always empty when the bottle came round, and was always refilled.

Projection The problem drinker says that he or she only drinks because outside forces or people pressurize them into it: 'I didn't really want the second bottle, but William insisted. It would have been rude to refuse.' As a generalization, men are more likely to use this excuse than women, as there is still the idea in some societies that it is weak to be unable to match other members of the party drink for drink. Women do also use the excuse, however, claiming that they drank too much because they thought it might be rude, or more and more often nowadays, because they are under pressure to show that they are equal to men.

Disassociation The drinker separates his or her drinking from the rest of their life, and when not in a drinking environment will, as the Italians say, 'put a stone on' this side of their behaviour. At home they are the worthy and loving spouse and parent. This dichotomy can reach its peak at the office party, but it can happen at any time when a potentially heavy drinker is freed from the constraints of his or her everyday environment.

One type of unusual behaviour after drinking is the idiosyncratic response. In these cases the drinker may become overemphatic, aggressive, even violent, after a single drink, which is certainly not enough to make them drunk in the conventional sense of the word. The usual explanation is that those who

become aggressive when they have been drinking are angry, but bottle up their anger; alcohol draws the cork and lets the anger out. If such people are extremely tense, even one drink may be disinhibitory enough to cause trouble.

It has been said that when aggression is a response to drinking, the drinker is suffering from such social, sexual or racial loss of self-esteem that they are permanently angry. Certainly, there are cultural differences in the response to alcohol: those who were born with a silver spoon in their mouths and doting parents are less likely to smash a glass in the face of the man beside them at the bar than is somebody whose life has been a battle, both financially and emotionally.

It is not unusual in hospitals to see a casualty whose only crime in the eyes of his attacker in the bar was to look at them in a certain way. This happened to Peter, who was drinking in a pleasant and smart pub in a university town with his student friends when an apparently sober man came across the bar and broke his jaw, knocking him to the floor with the words, 'I didn't like the way you were looking at me.'

14

Nutrition

Alcohol is such a ready source of calories that there is always the danger it will be taken instead of, rather than as well as, other food. One of the duties which for historical reasons went with my practice when I was a doctor in Norwich was to care for the down-and-outs when their health was causing concern to the authorities. I was called out at all hours of the day and night to see some homeless man or woman who had been found crumpled and comatose.

It does not need a medical qualification to realize that a scrawny derelict who has been drunk for months, if not years, is suffering from gross malnutrition. What is not often understood is that, unless precautions are taken, heavy drinkers who are taking a disproportionate amount of their calories as alcohol may, even if they are holding down a good job and living in comfortable surroundings, have a diet which is deficient in essential minerals, vitamins and other nutrients.

When assessing the effect of heavy alcohol consumption on overall nutritional balance, we need to take into consideration the diet itself, the absorption of the food and its subsequent digestion.

Too much alcohol can affect the absorption of all foods, but particularly vitamins and other micro-nutrients. This problem is the result not only of changes in gastro-intestinal motility – causing the drinker to suffer from the socially disruptive symptoms of flatulence, abdominal pain and even diarrhoea – but of more subtle internal changes that affect small intestinal permeability.

In the absorption of vitamins and minerals, it is important to maintain balance. Some of the flavonoids, for instance, will not be nutritionally available if essential vitamins are absent. An adequate amount of fat in the diet is vital if these vitamins are to be utilized, and an excess of one particular trace element may restrict the intake of another. Diet has to be both balanced and comprehensive, and if this equilibrium is lost, malnutrition may occur, even though the person may be of the correct weight for their age, sex and height.

The absorption of nutrients is hugely complex. Research has shown that alcohol enhances the absorption of some foods, including glucose and galactose. It has – provided there is no diarrhoea or damage to the pancreas – little effect on the absorption of fats, so long as there is an adequate intake of protein. There is always a temptation for the heavy drinker, whose appetite has probably been ravaged by his habit, to refuel on high-calorie fast foods that may be protein deficient. Heavy drinking inhibits the absorption of essential amino acids, the proteins everybody needs in order to stay healthy. Protein food is expensive food, so if a heavy drinker has become financially embarrassed by his habit, he may well be tempted to reduce his food bill by cutting back on meat and other protein-rich foods.

Deficiency in thiamine, one of the vitamin B group, could be considered the hallmark of malnutrition in the heavy drinker; it is an important cause of damage to both the heart and the nervous system. There are two parts to this problem: the diet of heavy drinkers is short of thiamine, and the little it contains is inadequately absorbed. If the liver is damaged by excessive alcohol, the thiamine deficiency may become severe, and the problem will be made worse still if alcohol-induced pancreatic disease, or changes to gastro-intestinal motility, have given rise to long-standing diarrhoea. However, moderate alcohol intake after suffering from an ulcer will do no damage whatsoever.

Thiamine is well represented in the standard British diet. Milk and orange juice are particularly rich in it, and it is also found in huge quantities in such exotic dishes as hard cods' roe and dressed crab or lobster. Fortunately, it is also found in potatoes, cereals, chicken and most red meats: 17 per cent of the average Briton's thiamine is derived from potatoes, 20 per cent from bread (white or wholemeal) and 13 per cent from meat. These are such staple constituents of the diet that it is easy to understand how someone whose appetite has been eroded by drinking could easily suffer from thiamine deficiency.

One recent change in the British diet has been an increasing fondness for oriental foods, which has resulted in more rice, and fewer potatoes, being eaten. This may exacerbate the problem. Rice in its usual polished state has had the thiamine removed, hence the frequency with which thiamine deficiency is encountered in the Far East. The heavy beer drinker is thus fractionally better off from a nutritional point of view if he ends his Friday night's drinking with fish and chips rather than curry and rice.

Another member of the vitamin B group, riboflavin or vitamin B2, is also frequently deficient in heavy drinkers. Unlike thiamine deficiency, this is not the result of poor absorption of the vitamin, which is found in milk, cheese, liver, meat and eggs, but simply because the diet of many heavy drinkers is lacking in these essential foods. Recent research showed that one in five heavy drinkers were deficient in riboflavin, which can cause problems with the eyesight and the skin, particularly sores at the corner of the mouth. The obvious treatment is to cut back to drinking the beneficial two to four glasses of red wine or its equivalent each day – but as riboflavin is not toxic, even in excess, and there are no contra-indications to its use, it might be a wise precaution to take it in pill form as well.

The importance of the vitamin folic acid has been underrated for years. When I was a junior doctor in the late 1950s my chiefs in the maternity unit where I was working insisted that all pregnant women should have additional doses of folic acid, but it has taken nearly forty years for their teaching to be accepted. Even now, despite government campaigns to persuade women who might become pregnant to take the vitamin before they conceive, few are doing so. Women still think that it is good enough to start once they know they are pregnant, but the crucial few days for the unborn baby are before the mother may be aware of the situation.

Folic acid is essential not only for pregnant women. Recent

work has shown that high levels of folic acid provide considerable protection against coronary heart disease, but random testing has found that 8 to 10 per cent of the population are deficient in folates, even though folic acid is widely dispersed in the food chain. Its principal sources are fresh green vegetables, the richer the green – as in broccoli and spinach – the better. Fruits are also a rich source, but, luckily for those who are not too keen on their greens, it is also found in liver and kidneys.

For people who need high blood levels of folates, either because they could become pregnant or because they are at increased risk of heart disease, increased dietary folate is not in itself enough to guarantee protection. Folic acid pills are necessary: the government recommends pills containing 400 micrograms a day unless there is a known history of folic acid deficiency, in which case they advocate 5 mg a day. My own view is that unless there is a contra-indication, such as a tendency to epilepsy, 5 mg daily (for which a doctor's prescription is needed in Britain) is safer.

It has been shown that no manipulation of the diet – such as giving the woman large helpings of broccoli with her kidneys and eggs several times a day – would provide enough folic acid to remove the danger of bearing a baby with physical defects. Pregnant women should not take liver, a source of folic acid, as the vitamins A and D also found in it can, if taken to excess, cause serious side-effects to mother and child.

Unfortunately, folic acid absorption is reduced by alcohol: the more that is drunk, the more difficulty the body has in absorbing the acid. To overcome the deficiency that can occur in people who drink, additional folic acid should be taken daily. I recommend to my patients – even those with whom I share a bottle of wine in the evening – that they should have the standard over-the-counter preparations of folic acid of 400 micrograms daily.

The importance of vitamins C and E as antioxidants is well-known. The association between the absorption and utilization of vitamin E and flavonoids is particularly strong. Vitamin C absorption is reduced if it is taken at the same time as alcohol: if fresh orange juice is mixed with vodka, some – but luckily not all – the vitamin C will be destroyed and the rest will be less well absorbed.

Maintaining a high vitamin C intake is therefore important for those who drink. Orange juice for breakfast, plenty of fresh vegetables (the skin of the potato and the area just beneath should be eaten) and fruit, particularly the citrus fruits such as oranges, lemons and grapefruit, as well as tomatoes and peppers – these are rich sources of vitamin C. The vitamin can also be taken in tablet form, but in enormous quantities these can have a laxative effect.

Moderate drinking does not affect calcium intake, and despite frequent statements to the contrary, research has shown that it has no deleterious influence on osteoporosis. Binge drinking also has no influence on calcium intake, but chronic heavy drinking does undermine the absorption of the mineral through the duodenum, part of the small intestine; this can be a factor in the development of osteoporosis – in such cases, any benefit from increased oestrogen production is nullified by the calcium deficiency.

Zinc is often recommended as a dietary supplement for heavy drinkers. It is known to have an important antioxidant action, and plays a part in many different enzyme systems, including alcohol dehydrogenase (ADH), which metabolizes alcohol. There has been little research into the absorption of zinc by drinkers, but there is scientific evidence that alcohol depletes the body's reserves of it. Zinc is not normally excreted in the urine in any great quantities, but alcohol does increase urinary excretion. Since the mineral is so important to the way in which the body deals with its alcohol, zinc supplements would not go amiss.

Unless taken in absurd quantities, zinc is not toxic, but it does compete with copper for absorption from the gut, so that a high zinc intake could cause a reduction in copper levels. Among good sources of copper are beer, cider and, surprisingly, dark chocolate. An adequate supply is essential to prevent anaemia and maintain strong, healthy bones.

It is widely believed that zinc helps to preserve the sexual drive and maintain men's fertility level; it is thought to play a part in ensuring the health of the sperm. In areas of the world where the diet is deficient in zinc, the young men are not only anaemic but puberty is delayed and the genitalia are under-developed; zinc supplements furnish them with the manhood they previously lacked.

The great value of the Mediterranean diet is that it is as inter-esting to eat as it is nutritious. It is beautifully balanced: the ordi-nary meals of the people who live in that region have developed as a result of custom coupled with availability, and have not been designed by a food scientist. Having said that, the Mediterranean emphasis on fish, fresh vegetables, fruit, cheese, olive oil, garlic and red wine could not have been better if it had been planned by an academic nutritionist.

15

The EU and the Eurobarometer

The European Union, ever anxious to know every detail of its people's lives, has conducted a comprehensive study of their drinking habits. Eurocrats have enquired into the amount the average man and woman in each of the member states drinks, the type of drink, when they drink it and for how many years they have enjoyed their particular tipple. The survey was carried out in 1988 as part of the twenty-ninth annual 'Eurobarometer', and the EU civil servants continue to monitor all changes in European behaviour, including alcohol consumption.

The gurus who tap the barometer of European drinking started with the assumption that those who lived in the Mediterranean countries drank wine daily and that most of the wine was taken with their meals. This premise, which is supported by some previous research, was that whereas in the warmer countries wine was the principal drink, in the chillier north beer was favoured and it was liable to be drunk standing by the bar, rather than sitting at the dinner table.

The Brussels survey hoped to find evidence for several widely held hypotheses. It has been assumed, for example, that the older a person becomes, the more likely they are to drink wine rather than beer. Increasing prosperity is claimed not to be the only cause of this apparent phenomenon; age brings with it relative stability, and wine as a regular drink suits their ageing demeanour better than the jolly barside party, fun though it may be on occasions.

The Eurocrats are not troubled by political correctness, and brazenly show that people of a higher educational level are more amenable to new influences, both on their cellar and their larder, and are more prepared to change their drink. Drinkers who have not had higher education tend to continue to consume the type of drink traditional to their class, race and background, whereas the neighbour who made it to university will be more adventurous.

The pivotal argument is that people from the higher social strata, particularly if they are well-educated but have relatively little cash, are likely to parade their cultural superiority by experimenting with – and professing to have a taste for – drinks from countries which hitherto have not been famous for their vineyards or breweries. Their esoteric tastes display an individuality which shows they have more to offer to society (and the dinner parties at which they are guests) than a gold credit card from an exclusive bank. It has been demonstrated that once a new drink has become established in a social group, the women and men who belong to the group are equally adept at accepting the change, and that, in consequence, the woman's drinking pattern tends to become more like that of the menfolk.

It is assumed that in all countries wine is consumed more often with food than is beer, but the survey has suggested that tastes in drinking are crossing the old territorial boundaries: in the northern countries the locals are drinking more wine, as well as more beer, and in the Mediterranean, beer is becoming more popular whereas wine is on the wane.

For the most part the changes have not been conducive to temperance: the new drink is taken 'as well as' rather than 'instead of'. In the wine-drinking areas, there has been some reduction in wine consumption to compensate for drinking more beer. This may well be a reflection of prevailing social mores. In the hotter southern countries drunkenness is culturally unacceptable, whereas in Russia the guest who is sober at the end of an evening may well be considered rather dreary and probably ill-mannered.

Neither brewers nor vintners should be too gloomy. Overall sales are going up, and the differences in consumption between one part of Europe and another are still substantial. The changes in spirit drinking are much less than those which affect wine and beer.

The heart of beer drinking is still north-west Europe:

Denmark, Germany, the Netherlands, Belgium, the United Kingdom and Ireland. In these countries beer drinking is still largely separate from eating, and is usually a daily event. In many parts of this country huge quantities of beer are drunk on Friday and Saturday evenings, followed very often by a session at Sunday lunchtime. Sometimes there will be another drinking session midweek, possibly to coincide with a darts or cricket match.

In northern Europe, and particularly in the Netherlands, Britain and Ireland, men going out for an evening's drinking and not intending to eat during the session will choose beer. However, despite the tradition of beer drinking – which has been maintained and even increased – the northern Europeans are not slow at adapting. In the thirty years after 1960 the consumption of wine per head of the population doubled in Germany, tripled in Belgium and Ireland, and increased sixfold in Denmark and the United Kingdom.

We in Britain are reverting to our roots: archaeological finds suggest that in the heyday of the Roman Empire the British who lived near the estuaries, and therefore had access to supplies from abroad, drank wine as lustily as any in southern Europe.

"IF I'M DRINKING WINE I LIKE A PROPER GLASS"

The dank countryside of the Fens even supported a Roman vineyard at Ely in Cambridgeshire.

Medical research which suggests that red wine bestows greater health advantage than white on moderate drinkers is one of the factors encouraging red wine drinking and discouraging white wine drinking in the United Kingdom. In 1995 sales of red wine increased by 13 per cent whereas those of white wine fell by 2 per cent.

The EU researchers found that wine drinking in the southern European countries continues in the established mould: wine is consumed daily, and there is no danger that lunch or dinner, even in the most spartan inn, will not be accompanied by a jug of wine. In France, Italy, Greece, Spain and Portugal, wine is still considered an essential part of a meal and is no more expensive than a bottle of mineral water in Britain. Even though wine with meals is still expected in these countries, the consumption has decreased slightly since 1960. Beer consumption, on the other hand, has been increasing, as it has in northern Europe; in absolute terms, this increase is the same in both areas of Europe, but in relative terms the southern European change is the greater, and the difference in beer consumption between the two regions is diminishing. The consumption of beer in the Mediterranean countries has increased fourfold in the past thirty years (except in France, where their beer drinking per capita was initially rather greater).

Those who disapprove of alcohol as a matter of principle tend to overestimate the number of teetotallers, whereas those who would like to keep the drinking tradition alive are inclined to underestimate the numbers of those who never drink. The EU reported in its extensive survey that 10 per cent of all men and 20 per cent of the women said they never drank alcoholic liquor. Just what people mean by 'drinking' can be difficult to interpret: if Granny has half a glass of sherry at Christmas to be companionable, how would she have filled in the form?

The lowest number of abstainers were found in Germany and Denmark, and perhaps surprisingly, the highest proportion was found in Portugal, Spain and Ireland. There are gender differences overall, as well as differences from one country to another. Belgian women are the lustiest northern drinkers, whilst Greek women drink less than those from other southern European countries. In both Greece and Portugal, the difference between the numbers of abstemious males and females was even greater: four times as many Greek women as men do not drink at all, and in Portugal the difference is threefold.

In Europe as a whole, 90 per cent of all men take alcohol at some time or another; for 86 per cent of them this includes wine. Moreover, 87 per cent of all male drinkers include beer in their repertoire; this overall figure does not give an entirely accurate picture, however, as a higher proportion of northern drinkers will sample beer, should the occasion demand it, than will southern drinkers.

For women, the figures are slightly different: 80 per cent of women drink, but 91 per cent of these drink wine. The survey showed that it is hard to be dogmatic about female drinking patterns: there are fewer racial differences and it is even difficult to make a clear distinction between the northern and Mediterranean countries. In many cultures in Europe, beer drinking by women has only become socially acceptable in the last fifty years. As female emancipation has progressed, it has brought with it the sight of women happily drinking in bars alongside the men – but even so, only 40 per cent of women who drink said they drink beer. This reluctance to tackle beer was particularly common in the northern countries, where some of the older woman are still shy of drinking out of a pint mug and looking like 'one of the boys'. A very practical reason why women were reluctant to drink beer in the past was that it had a greater diuretic effect than wine, and the beer-drinking woman was shy about having to make too many trips to the lavatory, a consideration which doesn't worry the younger generation. The advent of the fashionable small bottle of beer with an attractive label is doing much to break down the prejudice about female beer drinkers.

It is tempting to attribute the so-called French Paradox to wine drinking. This is the theory, supported by statistics, which suggests that although French people smoke more than many other races, are remarkably indifferent to their fat intake and are not famous for the amount of exercise they take, they tend to live longer.

Attempts have been made to explain this by inferring that French geriatric medicine is less advanced, and the certification of death therefore less precise, than elsewhere in western Europe. This argument is refuted by studies which have shown that not only are fatal heart attacks less common in the Mediterranean countries, but also that proven coronary heart disease in the living is less of a problem than it is in northern European countries.

Subsequent research has shown that this phenomenon should in fact be referred to as the Mediterranean Paradox, as a very extensive survey in Greece has reported similar findings. Greek men drink more wine than Greek women, and throughout the Mediterranean countries men drink wine one and a half times more often than the women. The diet of fresh fruit, salads, vegetables, olive oil and particularly onion and garlic, together with the wine, contributes to coronary arteries relatively free of atheroma. The fresh, often locally grown, produce is rich in antioxidants such as vitamin E and carotenoids, as is the wine, and the absorption of these life-prolonging chemicals is facilitated by the fatty cheeses which are an essential part of the diet. Vitamin C is also an excellent antioxidant and has particular influence on heart disease in men.

If wine drinking is one of the reasons for southern Europe's relative freedom from cardiovascular disease, in Britain and Denmark men and women are both doing their best to emulate this. Although in most of Europe wine drinking is more established among older people than younger, there is an exception: in the United Kingdom a younger woman is twice as likely to have wine with her meal as her mother.

In other countries the figures are not so striking, and it will be interesting to see in years to come if this increase in wine drinking is reflected in a reduction in the coronary heart disease rate in women, which is beginning to resemble the male pattern. A few years after the menopause, women begin to show an incidence of cardiovascular disease similar to that of men – although evidence is accumulating from Britain and America that in women who drink moderate amounts of alcohol this cardiovascular deterioration is less marked.

The increase in beer drinking which has been noted in southern Europe is essentially a habit adopted by younger people, and may well be a consequence of the burgeoning holiday trade and the demand of northern Europeans to have their beer even when on holiday. Younger people's drinking style has also been studied in detail. This research has shown that different generations have different patterns of drinking. As might be assumed from watching tequila drinkers in Fulham slam their glasses and down their shots, younger people tend to drink more alcohol at a faster pace in the course of an evening's drinking than does the older generation, but they do not drink on so many evenings during the week. This pattern of drinking is ingrained in the life style of young northern Europeans, particularly men.

This also applies to beer drinkers in northern Europe: the younger people drink it less often than the older generations (except in the Netherlands), but when they do go out for an evening's drinking they consume far more. Binge drinking – heavy periodic drinking – is very much more dangerous than the moderate, regular consumption of alcohol, and increases the likelihood of some forms of cardiac disease which can lead to arrest or to strokes. Interestingly, research in Sweden has shown that binge drinkers who stick to wine are less at risk.

The EU survey leaves little doubt that drinking patterns are changing, and that these changes reflect the evolution of society in general, the influence of travel and universal television. However, the traditional differences between northern and southern Europeans remain, albeit perhaps a little less clear-cut.

It seems reasonable to suppose that wine drinking will continue to gain in popularity in northern Europe, and that this may in time reduce the incidence of heart disease. It is also probable that southern drinking habits, where alcohol is drunk with meals rather than while propped against a bar, will extend into those northern climes where binge drinking has been traditional. This should reduce the incidence of strokes and fatal cardiac arrhythmias. The disturbing news for northern Europe is that although in general people drink less often than their southern counterparts, their drinking is still too heavy. The trouble has been that drinkers have tended not to substitute one style of drinking for another but rather to add their new-found tastes to their existing habits.

For most people, alcohol in moderation is more likely to improve rather than damage their health. Because alcohol is dangerous in excess, its advantages are often overlooked.

Set yourself a limit before you start an evening's drinking.

Try to keep track of when and what you drink.

Avoid drinking on an empty stomach.

It is better to drink at meal times, or at any rate with some food. Snacks should be served when drinks are offered.

Be aware of the difficulties of measuring a drink when pouring one at home. Most home-poured gins and whiskies are at least double the tot provided by the local publican (see table on p. 9).

Drink slowly, and dilute spirits with at least as much water. This might shock the Scots but it would help their health.

16

Allergy

Lunches in the City of London have changed out of all recognition in the last ten years. Even the rank and file in the financial houses, who could not in the past have expected a business lunch, might at least have hoped for a couple of pints at the local pub. But even in these Calvinistic days, in every office, every day, someone needs to entertain clients and colleagues. The more senior the worker becomes, the more often this is necessary.

To one of my patients, a bank director whose job was to control his firm's lending to their larger clients, this aspect of the job, which most would have found a pleasure, was a misery. Allergy to alcohol blighted his City life, for every time this supremely important director had to drink red wine with his clients to show bonhomie, his joints swelled. The more stressful the meeting, the larger and more painful the joints became by the time he struggled home in the evening. After a single glass of red wine his fingers and hands became so swollen that he could not undo his shirt buttons without his wife's help, should he need to change before going out in the evening.

The banker consulted various rheumatologists, all of whom agreed that the polyarthritis was an allergic reaction to red wine – but much as they understood joints, they had little comprehension of City life. Their prescription of no red wine, no joint pains, would have been an easy one to follow in some professions, but not for the director of a City institution.

After trial and error, an appropriate mixture of pills – non-sedative antihistamines and an anti-inflammatory drug – was found which enabled the banker both to enjoy a glass of wine with his clients and to put himself to bed unaided. As in many such cases, the strength of the allergic reaction to the wine depended on his state of mind at the time. If all was going well at the bank and at home, the director might manage a glass or two of Château Lafite without trouble, whereas if there were storm clouds on the financial horizon, merely tasting a glass for his guests could be enough to trigger a reaction. Now that he is retired from the City – although he seems just as busy doing the things he enjoys – he can drink as much as the next man, and never needs a pill before he settles down to dinner.

Some patients seem determinedly wedded to old-fashioned antihistamines, as opposed to the modern ones prescribed for the director, but they do not mix well with alcohol, whether it is a factor in their allergy or not. Those such as Piriton or Phenergan cross the blood-brain barrier, so that although the runny nose, red eyes and itchy skin may improve after they have been taken, it is at a cost: the patient's temper will become shorter, concentration may lapse and they may nod off to sleep. Driving is not recommended for those taking these original antihistamines, as the patient's reactions are apt to become slower as they become drowsier.

The new antihistamines have so little effect on the brain's functions that pilots are allowed to fly when taking them, students can no longer blame them for poor exam results, and a drink can be enjoyed in the sure knowledge that cerebral function will not be appreciably impaired. It is said that the advent of such preparations as Triludan, Hismanal and Clarityn has enabled golfers previously stricken with hay fever to play eighteen holes at the height of the pollen season and still join the other players at the bar. Some of these modern antihistamines may react adversely with antibiotics and other substances, and have very occasionally been blamed for causing cardiac arrhythmias.

No one can deny that Italian wines, always robust, are becoming better and better. However, I thought when I wrote in *The Times* about an experiment carried out in California that they were generally agreed to be more liable than other wines to trigger an allergic response in vulnerable drinkers. Some Italian wines contain very large quantities of free histamines, which is one of the reasons why a minority of people find that drinking them causes a vicious headache. The Californian doctors recommended, apparently with great success, that patients who enjoyed half a bottle of Chianti but paid for it next morning with a splitting head should take Tagamet, cimetidine, before they dined. However, other experts doubt that histamine plays any part in causing a headache after drinking.

It should be added that the Italians politely but firmly denied that their wine contained any more free histamines than those of any other country, and complained that repeating the story was perpetuating only a myth.

This belief that Italian wines do contain more free histamines is certainly widely held, and is shared by Dr A. W. Frankland of Guys and St Thomas's Hospital, doyen of British doctors specializing in the treatment of allergy. Dr Frankland is in a very good position to study the effects of alcohol, as he has allergic rhinitis, the technical term for a periodically stuffed-up, runny nose. Dr Frankland suffers his nasal symptoms about two hours after drinking more than one glass of red wine. The attack of allergic rhinitis is heralded by a bout of sneezing and the ensuing nasal symptoms last for ten hours.

The study of allergic reactions to wine is inevitably complex, as there are more than six hundred different substances in wine which in Dr Frankland's opinion could cause trouble. In Dr Frankland's own case, for example, not all red wines have the same effect. A glass of Beaujolais causes no symptoms, but two glasses produce severe symptoms, and he can only manage a very small quantity of Italian red. On the other hand, some red wines cause him little trouble and he is able to share a bottle. Provided that the reaction is never dangerously severe, finding the right wine is a matter of trial, error and patience.

Although red wine is more likely to cause symptoms than white wine – and fortified wines are more troublesome than table wines – there are people who have an adverse reaction to some white wines, but can manage reds with impunity.

Hangovers are blamed for every headache following a night's

drinking. Very often they are indeed the cause. However, many patients who have a tendency to migraine will mistake this for a hangover. Anything that can induce a headache can cause migraine in a susceptible patient. The teaching on migraine is changing, however. It used to be thought that it was the tyramine in a substance that induced the headache. Now it is realized that though there are similar amounts of tyramine present in red and white wines, migraine is more often associated with red wine. It is now thought that the headache is more likely to be related to the flavonoids in red wine, the health-giving phenolics. Red wine contains twenty-four times more of them than white wine.

The flavonoids act as inhibitors of the enzymes that break down catecholamines, which are related to headaches. Other experts believe that these flavonoids in red wine, so useful in preventing heart disease, may cause migraine in vulnerable drinkers by increasing the blood levels of tryptamines, chemicals found in the platelets. In future when I write about the health-giving properties of Italian reds, I shall be careful to include a note to the effect that those sensitive to red wines may feel far from their best next morning, but their life span may have been lengthened. The same principle applies to those who suffer from drinking red wines from any other corner of the world, whether it is Chile, Spain, Hungary or elsewhere.

Some patients find that their asthma is made worse by alcohol, others that it is improved by a drink. One group of asthmatics, those for whom control of their wheezing is often dependent on steroids, are very occasionally sensitive to the sulphites in wine. Sulphites are produced as part of the natural fermentation process but are also added to wine to improve its quality by preventing oxidation; they do not represent any danger to the average drinker.

The patient's own opinion of their respiratory function is not always accurate. Many people who think that their wheeze is better after a drink only have this impression because the depressive effect on the higher cerebral centres means they are less aware of the discomfort. Although they may not notice the symptoms, scientific testing of the pulmonary function of some asthmatics shows that after alcohol they may breathe less well.

Some time ago I was consulted by a patient who was unaware that he suffered from wheezing and became short of breath after drinking. He found this out in very unfortunate circumstances. One night, after he had had only two, or at the most three, glasses of wine, he was struck by a careless driver while getting into his own car. The car drove off, but a passing police car stopped. Having been involved in an accident, he was routinely breathalysed. To his horror, the patient found that he could not blow up the bag, or half an hour later the machine at the police station. He offered the only explanation he could think of: he had had tuberculosis in childhood, for which reason he had spent some time in hospital, and whilst in the army he had suffered a crushed chest and a punctured lung. In an effort to placate the law, he volunteered his blood or urine, but both were refused and he was charged with failing to give a specimen of his breath. At the subsequent trial, vitalographs – which measure lung function and record any wheeze were produced which illustrated the effect on his respiration of even small quantities of alcohol. Both his wheeze and his lung function were consistently but uniformly reduced when he was given alcohol, even if it were disguised. Despite the efforts of his barrister and doctor, he was found guilty.

Conversely, there are asthmatics whose lung function is genuinely improved by a glass of alcohol. The effect of tranquillizers on patients who wheeze is well-documented: the bank director with the allergic polyarthritis is not the only person to notice that the symptoms of allergy are worse when they are tense. Because of its tranquillizing action, alcohol can alter a person's perception of the social situation to the point where it becomes no longer stressful enough to induce a wheeze.

In many people, the wheeze produced by alcohol intake can be prevented by taking a couple of puffs of sodium cromoglycate, such as Cromogen, beforehand. As in many cases of allergy, prophylaxis is better than seeking a cure. Sodium cromoglycate is also helpful for those who develop a runny nose from alcohol; it is supplied in a metered dose container.

There is the occasional very unlucky patient in whom allergy to alcohol is not a matter of suffering a runny nose, but of becoming seriously ill. One of Dr Frankland's cases illustrates this: the patient tends to get acute laryngeal swelling if she has even a sip of any alcoholic drink, and this causes acute breathlessness, which is frightening, and loss of voice for some hours, which is socially incapacitating. Fortunately, the symptoms can be entirely prevented if before any social occasion she takes some puffs from her Medihaler Epi-aerosol, which contains adrenaline.

As laryngeal oedema can be very sinister, even fatal, this patient would perhaps be well advised to steer clear of alcohol altogether. However, even if she adopts this resolution, she should still carry her Medihaler Epi-aerosol with her just in case she is caught out by some alcohol hidden in a sauce or trifle. The reaction to an allergen is not always the same: a sudden increase in sensitivity can spell disaster.

Like any other substance that can cause allergy, alcohol very occasionally induces anaphylactic shock, the most dangerous form of allergic response. Anaphylaxis is the sudden crippling reaction to an allergen in someone who has already been sensitized to it before the calamity strikes. In the mildest form of anaphylactic reaction, the sufferer develops a generalized itch, an actual swelling of the face and lips – which become bloated and waterlogged – nausea, vomiting and sometimes diarrhoea. They find breathing difficult, as there is swelling in the larynx and wheezing.

In its most dangerous form, most commonly found in people allergic to nuts or bee or wasp stings, shock supervenes within a matter of minutes. The victim may have a fit and become incontinent; they can lose consciousness and perhaps die from heart or respiratory failure or some other complication. There is always the possibility of long-term kidney or brain damage in those who recover. People known to suffer from severe allergy, particularly to nuts or bees, should always carry with them a form of adrenaline, such as the Epi-pen, which can either be self-injected or administered by others. Epi-pens are expensive, but who begrudges fifty pounds if it will save a life?

It is well known that asthma is made worse by strenuous exercise, particularly in cold weather, and there are good reasons for this. Less well known is the fact that the symptoms of other forms of allergy, including those relating to alcohol, can be aggravated, or in some cases actually induced, if the allergen is taken at the same time as the patient exercises. This unsettling phenomenon may be the result of an increased speed of circulation after exercise. In Dr Frankland's paper on the interrelationship of alcohol and allergy, there is a report of one such case where a man had five attacks of anaphylaxis: three were associated with jogging, one was when he ran to catch a flight and one was while playing tennis – on which occasion he had actually collapsed.

The cause of the anaphylaxis was not immediately obvious. Exercise was the obvious common denominator, but the patient was a health enthusiast and frequently took exercise without developing such worrying symptoms. Alcohol was also considered as a possible cause, but it was established that the patient drank regularly, almost daily, and frequently took exercise after drinking without suffering dire consequences. However, undaunted, Dr Frankland believed that there must be some association between alcohol, exercise and these attacks, and by careful analysis of the patient's story together with painstaking testing of different alcohols, he discovered that rum was the only drink to which his patient was allergic. The sufferer could enjoy any other drink with total impunity, and if he did not have rum he could happily have entered the marathon.

The individual nature of allergies is never more clearly demonstrated than in those related to drinking. It is not unusual to find people who are unable to drink certain red wines because they make them sneeze or their eyes water; others will have an allergic response to one make of gin, but not to another. Beer drinkers may find that they can drink some beers with impunity, but that others cause almost immediate gastro-intestinal troubles or a splitting headache. As with the patient whose allergy to rum was made worse by exercise, so there are those who only react adversely to alcohol if they are overtired or overstressed.

Many people will attribute a change of personality to a particular drink: they may claim that champagne makes them amorous, brandy aggressive and port somnolent. These sufferers claim that they are 'allergic' to a particular drink. However, they are only showing the response of a tense person to the disinhibitory effect of alcohol. At many functions where champagne is served, there are plenty of people of the opposite sex who may attract the disinhibited drinker; brandy is usually drunk at the end of a possibly awkward dinner; and by the time the port comes, the diner is half asleep anyway. Both brandy and port are notorious for giving headaches, but this is nothing to do with allergies, but with the congeners these drinks contain. There are variations in susceptibility to the congeners, but that is not a true allergy.

To anybody sensitive about their appearance, a rash or spots are particularly distressing, and these can be induced by alcohol. The most common skin change after drinking is the simple flush; this is usually no more than vasodilation, in which the blood vessels in the skin are dilated. In some people, this flush is not only caused by social embarrassment but may also be the result of an allergic response to the drink.

As well as a simple allergic flush, other patients show an urticarial reaction similar to nettle rash. In some parts of Britain and most of America, this urticarial rash is referred to as 'hives'. It can be the initial symptom of a more serious allergy to alcohol, but is usually a straightforward consequence of exposure to the histamine in alcohol; it can be treated with antihistamines. A minor manifestation of the problem is the feeling that the lips are slightly swollen after a few drinks; this too is often worse if social tensions affect the sufferer during the drinking. The few glasses shared with a critical boss or an examining in-law may make the rash worse and the lips feel tight and tingly. The symptoms can also be exacerbated by hyperventilation. None of these symptoms should be taken lightly and require investigation by a doctor.

No discussion of alcoholic flushing is complete without mention of the skin reaction in many Oriental peoples when they drink alcohol. People who are sensitive in this way frequently develop a pronounced flush, together with some swelling of the skin, after anything more than a very small intake, perhaps only a glass or two. This is because many Far Eastern peoples metabolize alcohol differently, as is explained in Chapter 7.

Another problem faced by those with allergic tendencies is that both yeasts and moulds are often among the substances that induce a reaction. In some patients this may prevent the enjoyment of Marmite, others are allergic to the yeast which causes thrush, and some cannot take as much as a sip of champagne without first raiding the pill cupboard to stave off the inevitable response. Perhaps the most common allergy to champagne is a wheeze, but some develop a rash.

Without yeasts, beer could not be brewed and grape juice could not be fermented to produce wine. The skin of a single grape may be home to more than ten million yeast cells. These cells are living organisms and, like all organisms, excrete their metabolic waste. It is the excreta of the yeast cells which causes the fermentation of the juice and turns it into wine. How ironic that the least attractive of physical functions should lead to the creation of the finest château wines!

The peculiarities of living in Britain have been summed up in two characteristics: warm beer and cold houses. The dangers of drinking beer too cold are very rare, but in the occasional instance very real. There is an epitaph in Winchester which records the death of a local worthy who was unlucky enough to die after drinking his beer too cold. The death occurred long before the days of refrigerators, for it is only since World War Two that British beer has been served ice-cold. The stonemason who carved the memorial unintentionally recorded for all time one of the features of allergic reactions. Any drink – it does not have to be alcoholic, and it certainly does not have to be beer –

can induce a significant reaction if served very cold to someone with this rare susceptibility. In its milder forms, the sufferer may feel that a cold drink does no more than make them cough, not realizing that a cough induced in this way is often a manifestation of a wheeze.

The local worthy probably died from an acute attack of asthma induced by a cold drink, and not, as the gravestone has implied for generations, from the beer. If someone is allergic to a particular drink, alcoholic or soft, and it is served cold, any respiratory response to it will be augmented. Children can be allergic to cola drinks and those containing tartrazine (such as some brightly coloured fruit drinks), but in asthmatic children an attack can be induced merely by a glass of ice-cold water.

Empty your glass before you allow it to be refilled.

Avoid drinking at both lunchtime and in the evening.

Flavonoids are more abundant in red wine and dark beers than in other drinks. It is this abundance which gives these drinks an advantage, but other drinks also have a health-giving value.

Not all wines, even if the same colour, have equal cardioprotective qualities; flavonoid content depends on the type of grape, the nature of the soil, climate and the way in which the wine is made.

17

Alcohol and young people

There is nothing new about under-age drinking. The behaviour of young drinkers has worried their elders for centuries, probably for all of the ten thousand years during which wine has been drunk. After the Industrial Revolution, the migration of people from the countryside to the towns produced an environment which encouraged anti-social behaviour amongst bored and disillusioned adolescents. The changes in urban housing after World War Two, including the development of massive housing estates, mainly of flats, and the disintegration of the inner-city communities, might have been expected to exacerbate the situation. However, under-age drinking is nowadays no more of a problem than it was at the beginning of the century. What has increased is the general public's awareness of problem as a result of television and mass-circulation newspapers, coupled with the fact that everyone now has a greater knowledge about health issues.

If there was under-age drinking now at the level which prevailed in the Edwardian era it would be the regular lead in every current affairs programme. At almost the same time as my father qualified as a doctor in 1907, the *Illustrated London News* described under-age drinking in London public houses. The reporters kept twenty-three pubs under close observation for four days; during this time they were visited by nearly eleven thousand minors under the age of sixteen. Many were small children, who though they were not allowed to buy a drink were frequently offered one as a 'treat'.

In the same year there was a remarkable coroner's case in Wandsworth, when a child aged three years and nine months was found to have died from chronic alcoholism. Even today it is not uncommon for children of this age to die from alcohol, but this has usually been an isolated incident of a child stealing a drink when the parents were not watching. The death of the child in these cases results from hypoglycaemia as a result of acute alcohol poisoning and not, as in the case of the three-year-old, from damage caused by persistent consumption.

"I DON'T KNOW WHAT THE YOUNGER GENERATION IS COMING TO..."

It is unlikely that any toddler today would die from chronic alcohol poisoning, and despite media reports which suggest the contrary, there was little change in the level of alcohol consumption amongst young people between 1980 and 1990. Two recent studies by the Department of Psychiatry at the University of Edinburgh analysed the drinking habits of fourteen to sixteen-year-olds, looking with particular interest into the social background of those who drink heavily. The definition of heavy drinking used in this investigation is not the standard one derived from the number of units of alcohol taken per week, but is instead based on the amount drunk during a session. The males were considered heavy drinkers if they had more than eleven drinks in any one session and the females if they had more than eight.

The popular image of the under-age drinker is that of the male 'lager lout', noisy, aggressive and drunken. This picture is incomplete in several respects. In particular, the study shows that more females than males are prone to drink alcohol to excess: 10.2 per cent of the girls and 9.6 per cent of the boys were classified as heavy drinkers. As female behaviour is usually less disruptive or aggressive than a male's, it is noticed less and therefore excites less comment.

The survey also showed that there is ignorance amongst young drinkers about alcohol and its properties and about the strengths of the various drinks they had been enjoying. There

was a widespread belief that a tot of whisky is more intoxicating than a pint of beer, whereas science shows that there is twice as much alcohol in a pint of average-strength beer. When they chose a drink, the teenagers were not influenced by its strength.

As would be expected, there were differences in the drinking patterns and home environment of the heavy drinkers when compared with those of their contemporaries. The research workers studied the motivations for drinking heavily. Females were more likely than males to drink to calm their nerves and relax, but males were three times more likely to think that drinking was beneficial to their health. The males also found alcohol much more of a support in meeting the opposite sex. Both sexes found that drinking greatly increased the chance that they would enjoy a party, and many of both sexes agreed that peer pressure was significant. In both males and females, curiosity was a factor in heavy drinking; and many were led into drinking by boredom.

As would be expected, the heavy drinkers were more likely to drink in the company of friends, particularly when members of the opposite sex were present, than when out with their parents or in the parental home. Conversely, the great majority who were lighter drinkers were more likely to have had their most recent drink at home.

Many female heavy drinkers correctly asserted that eating with drinking will slow down the effects of alcohol. They also believed that they were more intellectually alert after a drink, which is also true – although only as long as they do not have more than two drinks.

The Edinburgh report stresses that the overwhelming majority of these teenagers were not heavy drinkers, even though there was a great deal of illegal drinking. Although 38 per cent of those questioned admitted to buying alcohol illegally, there was no evidence to suggest that all those who were heavy drinkers would necessarily become problem drinkers, although there was obviously a risk.

In view of this risk of problem drinking in young people, the Portman Group – which, it should be remembered, is an organization funded by the drinks industry to encourage moderate, and discourage heavy, drinking – is constantly issuing advice to parents. It is the opinion of those who report to the Group that the most important influence on a young person's drinking style is their parents.

The Portman Group suggests that how much a parent drinks and how they behave when they are drinking will be noticed by their children and will probably set the pattern for their own drinking. It recommends that parents should neither exaggerate nor underrate the problems caused by heavy drinking, and should talk to their children without attempting to scare them. If there is drinking in the household, it should be made a natural, enjoyable part of the life-style for everyone. However, children should not be encouraged to drink, but should be allowed to have a taste if they want it – it should never become a big issue. Even if a teenager does come home drunk, it is pointed out, the situation is unlikely to be improved by preaching.

According to the Edinburgh research workers, 'teenagers who are heavy drinkers are more likely to use alcohol as a means of helping them to relax, to socialise, for curiosity, to relieve boredom and because their friends all drink'. It is not surprising that they are also more likely to indulge later in other forms of undesirable behaviour, such as using illicit drugs and smoking.

Giving alcohol to a child under five years old is illegal, and parents should not leave it lying around where a young child might happen upon it.

Parents are always concerned that their behaviour may have contributed to any excessive teenage drinking that occurs in their families. Parents do have influence, but to what extent this is a reflection of different customs and life-styles – not necessarily related to income – is uncertain. Parents' views are often representative of those of the group in which the family moves. The statistics suggest that heavy drinkers had more permissive parents than light drinkers, and that they felt their parents would be less likely to object if the boys drank when at a party and the girls when they went out for a meal. The influences acting on a young person are complex, and have now been further confused by the introduction of 'alcopops', which taste innocuous but pack a punch. The teenagers' approach to alcohol is fashioned by the subtle interplay between their inherited personality, the impact of the behaviour of their parents and that of their contemporaries.

18

Alcohol as medicine

The vine is symbolic of so many aspects of life: the changing seasons and rebirth, fertility, religious faith and health. If anyone doubts the significance of the grape to health, they should join a ward round. On nearly every bedside table a bunch of grapes lurks between the get-well cards and the hospital jug of water. Why do visitors always instinctively feel they have to bring a pound of grapes?

Not that some of the patients might not have preferred the grapes after fermentation into a bottle of wine. In his *La Physiologie du Goût*, Brillat-Savarin quotes a heavy drinker who was offered grapes:

'No, thank you,' he said, 'I am not in the habit of taking my wine in the form of pills.'

Wine in one form or another has always been part of the medical armoury, and in his book *L'Art de Cuisine*, Toulouse-Lautrec even offers the recipe for a cure for chronic bronchitis. This combines two traditional remedies, the prophylactic power of garlic and the anti-infective properties of alcohol:

Chop a pound of garlic, put it into a litre measure of old Port, and let it macerate for twenty days. Begin with half a liqueur glass every evening before the soup course, then slowly increase the dose to one or two liqueur glasses.

Wine was used in ancient times to treat the sick and infirm, long before Toulouse-Lautrec held court in Parisian café society. Popular histories claim that it was wine which enabled the Roman army to conquer Europe. The legionaries remained healthy and infection-free while their enemies succumbed to every epidemic and their wounds festered.

Since the time of the ancient Egyptians, alcohol has been used medicinally to treat internal complaints. The ancients used wine mixed with a wide variety of medicinal compounds that at the time were considered useful in treating diseases. Physicians such as Galen and Paulus of Aegina made a particular study of these ingredients. Centuries later, doctors were still adding herbal remedies to their wine: the claret might have been laced with digitalis for the heart or colchicine for gout. Medieval physicians fortified wines not only with extracts of meat, but were also

" YOU GET THIS MADE UP AT THE OFF-LICENCE "

happy to throw into the cask cocoa, quinine or straight medicines such as ipecacuanha.

This last was also a favourite drug of the Victorians, who used it as an expectorant to loosen a cough. It has the side effect of inducing nausea and vomiting if taken to excess, a sure way of making certain that the invalid did not over-indulge in the remedy. In this way the Victorian doctors not only devised a useful cough medicine but foreshadowed the practice of modern drug companies, who sometimes incorporate an antidote into a preparation that should not be taken in excess.

In medieval times, one of the tricks of the monks was to mix the less palatable concoctions with alcohol so that the taste was bearable. This monkish subterfuge continued until recent times, for even within living memory there was an alcoholic base to many medicines, despite the tradition that if a medicine was not unpleasant it was ineffective.

The custom of enriching wines with medicines still continues. Until recently, my own home town of Norwich had a prosperous business which manufactured Wincarnis, a wine fortified with protein extracts so that it could be recommended for those who were anaemic. Many of my highly respectable Nonconformist patients never realized why they felt so much better for their Wincarnis: it was not, as they thought, because the wine was boosting their haemoglobin, but because the alcohol in it relaxed their psyche. Wincarnis was not the only wine which contained iron in an effort to combat anaemia: vinum ferricum, an iron and sherry mixture, was listed in the British Pharmacopoeia within the lifetime of many older doctors still practising – it was guaranteed to bring roses to the cheeks of the most wan of minister's wives.

The Romans used alcohol not only as a drink that had medicinal benefits, but also as a dressing, the legionnaire's equivalent of surgical spirit. In utilizing the antiseptic qualities of wine, Roman soldiers were merely following the guidance laid down by Hippocrates five hundred years earlier. Galen also recommended wine as a dressing; indeed, his advocacy of wine in general, which was accepted by the ever-expanding Christian church, is credited with keeping it in the forefront of medical opinion once the Roman influence had started to decline.

Wine was an essential part of surgical practice in the Middle Ages. It was recommended for removing debris from a wound, as an antiseptic, and as a poultice. Battle wounds were disinfected by wrapping the injured limb in a poultice saturated in wine, and the wine, when mixed with various oils, was also a favoured cleansing agent. In my grandfather and father's day, surgical spirit was considered an excellent way of decontaminating a wound. Until the modern medicated soaps became available, every casualty trolley had its bottle of spirits, accompanied by a galley pot – a small metal cup without handles. Alcohol is now mainly used as a disinfecting agent for skin and hard surfaces.

Today, science has shown that the Romans and Greeks, as well as the medieval monks, were right in their belief that alcohol in small doses increases resistance to many infections, including the common cold. The hot toddy – the best recipe is whisky, lemon, cloves, hot water and honey – is a traditional cure for minor chills and colds. It is easy to dismiss the toddy as being effective only because it makes the patient feel better, but there is a possible physiological explanation for its use. It was first suggested about forty years ago that when someone becomes very chilled there is vasoconstriction of the nasal mucosa as well as of the skin. The vasodilation which follows the hot toddy increases the blood supply to the nose as well as to the skin. The argument, which is hard to prove or disprove, was that a healthier circulation to the nasal mucosa made it less likely that the drinker would fall prey to the common cold, or if the cold was already established, to secondary bacterial infection.

Too much alcohol lowers resistance by undermining the immune system. This is a common phenomenon that most of us have observed at some time or another. Someone who is foolish enough to drink to excess frequently finds that, a day or two after the party, a cold which was lurking in the background bursts forth; the viruses of any friends met while drinking have found their way to attack a new and enfeebled host.

Hippocrates also recommended wine for its cooling qualities. Since alcohol causes vasodilation, it does not warm the cockles of the heart but chills the marrow. Hippocrates recommended – and doctors for many centuries, including the fashionable Roman physician Galen, followed his advice – that alcohol should be prescribed for those with a fever.

Hippocrates' observation that alcohol chills the body is the very reason why it should not be given to those who have been lost in the snow and may already be suffering from hypothermia. The time for the drink is when the frozen traveller is back indoors with his or her back to the fire; the vasodilation is then helpful, because it exposes a greater proportion of the circulating blood to the warmth of the flames. (See Chapter 7, Effects of Alcohol).

Although there may just be some basis for administering a hot toddy, the prescription of brandy for all and sundry after an accident can be dangerous, despite its use in these circumstances in films and plays. The practice of giving strong drinks to people who were injured, or about to undergo an operation, dates from the time when there was no anaesthesia and the only relief the patient could expect was that provided by the brandy bottle. If the dispenser of the brandy can be certain that there is no physical injury, either internal or external, brandy can be a useful sedative. But if there is any question of injury which may need anaesthesia and surgery, the offer of anything by mouth while waiting for the ambulance – be it a hot cup of tea or a medicinal brandy – can be a lethal mistake.

One of the ideal times to bring out the brandy or whisky bottle is after an emotional rather than a physical trauma. On these occasions, the secret is not to overdo the medicine: a stiff double and a family's morale will be boosted – too much, and the disinhibitory effect of alcohol may exacerbate the initial problem and everybody's reaction to it. It is often difficult enough to deal with a household that is emotionally upset, frightened or grieving; they become infinitely more difficult if they have had a little too much to drink.

Part of the confusion about the treatment of shock, which has led to this hazardous use of alcohol, is that many people do not know that there are two different types. Physiological shock is often the result of blood or fluid loss, although it can also follow a heart attack or acute abdominal emergency; it leads to a low blood pressure, sweating, clammy skin, a rapid feeble pulse, breathlessness with shallow breathing and possibly collapse. Psychogenic shock, which is what most people understand by 'shock', may manifest itself in physical symptoms, but the basic cause is alarm, misery and anything which can induce sudden emotional upset.

In the nineteenth century wine was also added to water to combat cholera; the mixture was a fairly heady one, being one-third wine, two-thirds water. As the cholera organism is only likely to cause infection when it is present in very large quantities, the dilution of the contaminated water as well as the antiseptic qualities of the wine must have been helpful.

The 'hair of the dog' is another well-established practice, but not one that is currently fashionable in medical circles. The term is derived from the belief that a dog bite would get better if the victim plucked a hair from the culprit and swallowed it. The fact, regrettably known to every alcoholic, that alcohol after a heavy night's drinking does resuscitate the battered senses is perhaps one of the reasons for the success for more than a hundred years of D. R. Harris and Co's Original Pick-Me-Up. Harris's is a London chemist's shop, established for over two hundred years, tucked away in St James's Street amongst the smartest clubs.

For a century, clubmen jaded after a night's heavy drinking have called in to Harris's to beg a spoonful of the magic liquor, to be taken in water, so that they may derive the benefits of what the label describes as 'a rapid restorative'. Although the dose tastes disgusting to those who are unused to it, the manufacturers are not modest about its qualities:

> ... a splendid reviver in the morning, and taken shortly
> before lunch and dinner also serves as an excellent aperitif ...

People who live further from the centre of London, too far away to cadge a spoonful regularly, can arrange for a bottle to be sent to them. The label on the bottle reveals the truth about the mixture: it contains a subtle blend of ingredients designed to settle the digestion, some cloves to soothe the system and a drop or two of spirit to lift the mood. Do not be tempted to assess its 'nose' before it is diluted; it will bring tears to the eyes.

Eighteen hundred years after the Roman soldiers were kept healthy by wine as they defeated the barbarians and marched through Europe, Australia was colonized. The successful settlement of the continent without unacceptable loss of life was in part made possible by the medicinal qualities of wine.

It had been discovered in the early convict ships that if wine was issued to the prisoners bound for Botany Bay they were more likely to arrive in good heart and ready to work. So great was the improvement in the health of the convicts, and their relative freedom from infection, if they were on a ship where wine had been drunk, that the ships' surgeons refused to sail unless there were adequate provision of what they called 'the necessaries': this term included not only rice, tea, sugar and all the other contents of the larder, but also wine.

Once it became the responsibility of the ship's doctor to dispense the wine, teetotallers were not tolerated, as they were considered a menace to the others. The association between medicine and wine making became established in the culture of Australia and the minds of Australians.

Many of the earliest winefields in Australia were established by doctors, and even today some of the most famous vineyards and distilleries are still run by physicians and surgeons; the medical profession in Australia is responsible for 60 per cent of the grape harvest. When the ship's surgeon retired from the sea and established his practice ashore, he usually planted vines so that he could continue to dispense the medicine he had found most useful during his seafaring days. This was no different from the tradition in Victorian Britain that the doctor had a senna bush growing in his garden so that he could provide the locals with the aperients on which they relied.

Dr Philip Norrie, whose ancestors planted a vineyard, is one of Australia's 160 doctors still involved in wine production. He has made a special study of the health of the convicts on the prison ships, the establishment of the Australian wine industry and brandy distilling, and its relationship to the medical profession.

Dr Norrie reports that, in the First Fleet, only twenty-four of the 775 convicts died. The chief ship's surgeon Dr White attributed these excellent statistics to 'the liberal use of malt and good wine', and expressed particular gratitude to Lord Sydney, Principal Secretary of State, and Mr Nepan, the Under Secretary, for their humanity in ensuring that adequate supplies were available. The second fleet, which did not have the advantage of surgeon White and his influence with Lord Sydney, fared less well: 274 of the 965 convicts actually died on the journey, and many more had to be hospitalized as soon as they arrived in Port Jackson.

The early lessons were ill-learnt, and transportation became notorious for its death rate. Thirty years after Dr White's voyage, a government inquiry established that much of the mortality could be laid at the door of the ships' captains, who were withholding the wine ration and selling it en route in Cape Town or Rio. The government decreed that in future the wine should be in the care of the ship's doctor, who should not be responsible to the captain for its dispensation.

For thousands of years alcohol has been the tranquillizer of choice. The tranquillizers provided by the pharmaceutical industry have always been difficult to administer: they should be used only for short periods of time, to tide people over a difficult patch. They have another use: they can be taken when a patient knows that they will have to confront a difficult day – some cardiologists feel that they are now under-prescribed for this use. This reluctance on the part of doctors to recommend tranquillizers is understandable, however, as they can be addictive. Some people could easily become reliant, as there is a temptation to start taking them more and more readily in less and less stressful conditions.

The same worry applies to the use of alcohol to relieve stress. In many situations, drink is invaluable and supports many people through difficult and tense moments. No one would criticize the glass of whisky taken after an emotional shock, but to depend on increasingly large doses as a means of surviving the rigours of a heavy social life or a stressful working or domestic life has real dangers.

The use of alcohol in small quantities to restore morale is an ancient habit. François Rabelais (*c.* 1494–1553) neatly summed up the value of wine as a tonic:

> The juice of the vine clears the mind and the understanding, banishes sadness, imparts gladness and jollity.

In this, Rabelais was only reiterating the views of Hippocrates, who advocated the use of white wine to treat dropsy. This would not meet with twentieth-century approval, but Hippocrates did suggest that gaiety and a few drinks could banish the 'sad humour' and were the only effective treatment for mental diseases. John Brown (1735–1788) specifically advocated the drinking of claret to ward off fatigue and depression. Times have changed, however: seriously depressed patients need specific treatment, not a stiff drink, but the occasional medicinal use of alcohol can be justified in most cases. The exceptions are those who suffer from some psychiatric and neurological disorders which exclude them from drinking.

Alcohol used in moderation is the oil that lubricates social life by increasing the extroversion of even the most inhibited. The value of a regular evening drink to the over-tired worker after a demanding day is hard to estimate, but it probably has an influence on the decreased incidence of cardiac disease, and the reduction in overall mortality. Alcohol is able to halt the niggling anxieties and resentments that so often accrue during the day; this property makes it, when taken in strict moderation, a valuable aid in alleviating transitory stress.

People who rely upon their evening drink to restore their morale, as well as those who condemn the practice, should remember the words of G. K. Chesterton:

The dipsomaniac and the abstainer both make the same mistake: they both regard wine as a drug and not as a drink.

The self-mocking comment of heavy drinkers, delivered with a wink as they take their fifth glass, that it is 'just for medicinal purposes' is not supposed to be believed by their cronies, nor should it be. But there are times, 2,500 years after Hippocrates, when his theories do still apply.

Glossary

Adenoma A growth, usually benign, with a gland-like structure.

Aetiology The study of the origins of a disease or condition.

Affective disorder The technical term used to describe an abnormal mood, whether depression or mania.

Alcohol dehydrogenase (ADH) An enzyme which metabolizes alcohol.

Alcoholic dementia Intellectual and mental deterioration as a result of excessive, prolonged alcohol intake.

Allergy Hypersensitivity induced by exposure to a particular allergen; for instance, hay fever, induced by pollen.

Allopurinol A drug which increases the excretion of uric acid and thereby prevents attacks of gout.

The American Nurses' Survey Ongoing survey of the health and life-style of 87,526 female nurses.

Anaphylaxis and anaphylactic shock Anaphylaxis is an exaggerated response to a substance to which a patient is sensitive. When the reaction is so severe that the patient collapses it is described as anaphylactic shock.

Angina Chest pain caused by coronary heart disease; classically, but not invariably, felt behind the breast bone and radiating into the left shoulder and down the left arm.

Antabuse A drug which produces nausea, sweating and faintness if someone who has taken it then drinks alcohol.

Anti-coagulant A preparation taken to make a patient's blood less likely to clot.

Antihistamine A drug which counters the action of histamines and is therefore useful in treating allergies.

Antioxidant A substance which inhibits oxidation within the tissues. Oxidation is an essential process, but one which has dangers as well as benefits.

Arthroscopy The study of the inside of the joint by the use of an endoscope, an illuminated tube which allows a doctor to look into the joint space.

Asthma A disease marked by recurrent bouts of wheezing, coughing and breathlessness due to constriction and swelling of the lining of the bronchi.

Atheroma A fatty substance deposited on the inside of the arteries in people with arterial disease.

Atherosclerosis The deposition of a fatty substance on the inside of an artery. The fatty plaque contains cholesterol and has some of the appearance of lumps of porridge.

Atrial fibrillation An irregular action of the heart when the chambers are no longer beating in sequence; the large pumping chambers of the heart, the ventricles, are out of step with the collecting chambers, the atria.

Benign hypertrophy The enlargement of a gland or other part of the body when the increase in size is not due to a malignant condition.

Benzodiazepines A well-known group of drugs which has tranquillizing and sedative properties, e.g. valium and mogadon.

Biliary Related to bile, the fluid produced by the liver before flowing into the intestine.

Blackouts In alcoholics, an inability to remember anything which happened during the drinking bout.

'Brewers droop' Impotency as the result of having had too much to drink.

Carcinogen A substance which can induce malignant (cancerous) change. Hence *anti-carcinogen* is a substance which inhibits this effect.

Cardiac arrhythmia Any variation from the normal rhythm of the heart-beat.

Cardiomyopathy A disease of the heart muscle; divided into *hypertrophic, restrictive,* and *dilated* types. Cardiomyopathy may be the result of excessive alcohol intake for a great many years.

Cardio-protective Anything which gives benefit or protection to the heart.

Carotenoid Naturally occurring substances such as Beta-carotene, a precursor of vitamin A which is found in carrots, peppers and many other vegetables, which have antioxidant powers. They give the characteristic bright colour to many vegetables and leaves; the higher the colour, the higher the content of carotenoid.

Catechin A flavonoid found in red wine.

Catecholamines Organic compounds containing nitrogen.

Cimetidine A drug used to treat duodenal and gastric inflammation.

Cirrhosis A disease of the liver, marked by progressive destruction of liver cells. Contrary to popular belief, not all cirrhosis is the result of heavy drinking.

Civil Servant Survey A survey reviewing the health and life-style, including drinking habits, of 1,422 civil servants over ten years.

Colchicine A drug used in the treatment of gout.

Congeners Complex organic chemicals which give alcoholic drinks their distinctive colour and taste. They are responsible for much of the hangover.

Coronary heart disease Disease of the arteries of the heart with the result that the heart muscle is deprived of an adequate supply of oxygen and other nutrients.

Cutaneous nerves Sensory nerves supplying the skin.

Diastole The stage in the timing of the heart rhythm when the chamber is relaxed. *Diastolic* is therefore used to describe the blood pressure in the arteries when the pumping chambers of the heart are relaxed and filling.

Delirium tremens An acute mental condition marked by delirium, trembling and great excitement, anxiety, mental distress, sweating and chest pain. It affects heavy drinkers who suddenly stop drinking or cut their intake drastically.

Sir Richard Doll Eminent epidemiologist, whose speech in 1991 helped to influence medical opinion in favour of moderate alcohol intake.

Duodenum The first portion of the small intestine, so called because it is about twelve finger-breadths in length.

Dysentery Inflammation of the intestines, especially that of the colon, attended by pain and frequently with mucus and blood present in the stools.

Dysphagia Difficulty in swallowing.

Endocrine The glands which secrete hormones.

Epigastrium The part of the abdomen immediately between the breast bone and the area above the belly button.

Ethanol The technical term for alcohol.

FDA Food and Drug Administration, the US body which controls national policy in relation to both.

Fibrinogen One of the proteins in the blood which is involved in the clotting process.

Flavonoid A group of antioxidant, vitamin-like substances similar to the carotenoids.

Foetal alcohol effect Babies born to women who drink heavily may be slightly smaller, and less bright, than their contemporaries without having the physical stigmata of the Foetal alcohol syndrome (*q. v.*).

Foetal alcohol syndrome A rare condition seen in the children of women who drink heavily during pregnancy. There is increased risk of miscarriage and birth defects. The baby is classically small and mentally retarded, with a small head, tiny jaw, cleft palate and a pixie-like appearance.

Folates The salts of *folic acid* (*q. v.*).

Folic acid A vitamin found in a wide variety of foods. It has antioxidant qualities and is essential for bone marrow function. High levels of folic acid are associated with a reduction in the incidence of foetal abnormalities and coronary heart disease.

Framingham Study An ongoing study of the health of the population of a small town in the United States.

Free radical Unattached electrons with strong oxidizing powers which are potentially damaging to healthy tissue.

French paradox Phrase coined by Professor Serge Renaud to highlight France's low cardiac mortality rate relative to French consumption of alcohol, tobacco and fatty foods.

Galactose Obtained from lactose or milk sugar by the action of an enzyme.

Gall bladder Pear-shaped reservoir for the bile on the undersurface of the liver.

Gastrin A hormone produced in the stomach which is important in digestion as it stimulates the flow of gastric juices.

Gastritis Inflammation of the stomach.

Gastroenterologist Doctor who specializes in diseases of the stomach and intestine.

Gastro-intestinal Anything relating to the stomach and intestine.

Gout A condition characterized by an excess of uric acid in the blood and by attacks of acute arthritis caused by its deposition in the joints.

Gynaecomastia Enlarged male breasts.

Haemorrhagic stroke A stroke caused by bleeding from a cerebral blood vessel.

Hallucinations Perceptions not founded upon objective reality. Hallucinations can come in many different forms, including auditory, gustatory, olfactory and visual.

HDL (High Density Lipoprotein Cholesterol) Cholesterol is a blood fat composed of different constituents; the HDL Cholesterol is cardio-protective.

Helicobacter pylori Small bacterial organism which lives in the stomach and is related to duodenal and gastric ulceration.

Hepatitis Inflammation of the liver.

Histamines An amine which occurs in all animal and vegetable tissues. It is a powerful dilator of the capillaries and a stimulator of gastric secretion.

Hodgkin's disease A malignant disease involving the lymph nodes, spleen and, in general, lymphoid tissues.

HRT Hormone Replacement Therapy.

Hypertension The technical term for high blood pressure.

Hypoglycaemia Level of glucose in the blood below the normal limit.

Ipecacuanha A drug which, when taken in small quantities, loosens a cough. If taken in larger quantities it induces vomiting.

Ischaemic stroke A stroke as a result of the obstruction of a cerebral blood vessel by a thrombus or embolus (a clot).

Korsakoff's syndrome A psychosis which is the result of chronic alcoholism. Its characteristics include memory loss and disorientation. Confabulation, in which the patient makes up stories to compensate for the forgetfulness, is an early feature of the disease.

Larynx The voice box.

LDL (low density lipoprotein cholesterol) This is the pernicious portion of the cholesterol. A high level of LDL is a bad prognostic sign.

Lymphatic system A system of vessels which drains the lymph fluids from the body's tissues and filters the fluid in the lymphatic glands.

Lymphoma Any tumour made up of lymphoid tissue, of which *Hodgkin's* (*q. v.*) is one variety.

Malabsorption The inadequate absorption of nutrients from the digestive tract.

Marchiafava-Bignami disease A rare neurological disease which affects heavy drinkers. Patients become disorientated and, in time, demented. It used to be thought to be confined to drinkers of 'rough' red wine, but it is now known that it can affect any heavy drinker.

Medullary The central portion of a gland or other organ.

Meta-analysis A widespread analysis.

Micro-nutrients Nutrients which are required by the body only in very small quantities, such as copper or selenium.

Microsomal ethanol oxidising system A subsidiary system for the metabolism of alcohol.

Motility Movement. Thus sperm motility is the ability of sperm to swim, gut motility is the passage of intestinal contents through its system.

MRI Magnetic Resonance Imaging; a means of viewing in three dimensions parts of the body which would otherwise be inaccessible. No radiation is involved.

Mucosa The mucous membrane that lines the cavities of many of the hollow structures of the body.

NSAID (non-steroidal anti-inflammatory agents) Drugs which reduce inflammation and are therefore the standby in the treatment of the pain of rheumatic and other inflammatory diseases. They inhibit the production of prostaglandins, the natural chemicals which produce inflammation.

(Peripheral) Neuropathy Neurological disease affecting the peripheral, as opposed to central, nervous system.

Occlusion A blockage, such as might be found in a vessel or other hollow organ.

Oedematous Swollen with fluid; the old term was 'dropsical'.

Oesophagus The gullet, which extends from pharynx to stomach.

Oestradiol One of the oestrogen hormones (see below).

Oestrogen Hormone secreted by females.

Osteoarthritis A degenerative form of arthritis which is common in old age or in those whose joints have been subjected to excessive wear as a result of disease or injury.

Osteoporosis The loss of the matrix, or structure, of the bone so that it becomes very brittle and hence liable to fracture.

Pancreas A large, elongated gland behind the stomach; it is the largest gland in the body involved in digestion.

Pancreatitis Inflammation of the pancreas.

Parotid glands The glands in front of and below the ear which secrete saliva. It is these glands which are enlarged in cases of mumps.

Pathogenic Any condition which gives rise to disease.

Peristalsis The rhythmical relaxation and contraction of the guts which propels the contents downwards and onwards.

Phenolics Chemicals derived from phenol, an organic chemical.

Plaque A raised, usually flat, lump.

Platelets Small particles in the blood which are an essential part of the clotting mechanism.

Polyarthritis An arthritic process which affects more than one joint.

Porphyria An hereditary, metabolic disorder which is associated with intermittent dementia. Its most famous victim was George III.

Potency In the medical sense, a man's ability to achieve a strong enough erection for penetration.

Prostaglandins The natural chemicals which cause inflammation.

Purines Nitrogenous compounds produced by the metabolism of certain proteins such as those found in liver and kidneys, sardines and vegetables of the pea family. A diet which produces large quantities of purines is liable to precipitate gout.

PVPP One of the chemicals used to hasten the maturing process in the manufacture of wine.

Pylorus The outlet of the stomach.

Quercetin A flavonoid commonly found in red wine, garlic and onions. Thought to have anti-carcinogen properties.

Resveratrol A flavonoid found in large quantities in red wine. Helps to reduce platelet stickiness, thereby reducing the risk of coronary heart disease and heart attack. Resveratrol has recently been shown to have anti-carcinogenic properties too.
Riboflavin Also known as vitamin B2. Can be found in milk, liver, kidney, eggs and various algae.
Rutin Flavonoid found in red wine.

Safe limits The government recommendation as to the amount of alcohol it is safe for most people to drink without any risk of endangering their health.
Sialadenosis Swelling of the salivary glands.
Spider naevi Enlarged blood vessels in the skin, with smaller blood vessels leading from it. The enlarged blood vessel resembles the body of a spider, the smaller vessels its legs.
Steatorrhoea Faeces which contain an abnormally large quantity of undigested fats.
Steroid/non-steroid A group of hormones either produced in the body or artificially as a drug. These hormones include such well-known substances as cortisone and the sex hormones.
Systole The stage in the timing of the heart's rhythmic beat when the main pumping chambers of the heart are contracting. *Systolic* blood pressure is therefore the pressure in the arteries when the heart is contracting.

Terroir In wine making, the environment produced by the climate, the soil and the landscape.
Testosterone Hormone which determines masculine characteristics.
Thiamine Vitamin B1; found in beans, green vegetables, sweet corn, egg yolk, liver, corn meal and brown rice.
Tophi (Gouty) A deposit of urates found in the tissues around joints or,

for instance, in the cartilage of the ear. They are chalky in appearance.

Total cholesterol The overall cholesterol level, including both high and low density lipoprotein (*q. v.*).

Triglyceride Another blood fat. Raised levels of triglycerides are associated with an increased risk of cardiovascular disease.

Tryptamine A chemical related to the pancreas.

Ultrasonography The science of examining the inside of the body by using sound waves (as opposed to X-rays).

Unit The standard measurement of alcohol, used for example in the definition of the government's *safe limits* (*q. v.*).

Urates The salts of uric acid.

Uric acid The breakdown product of the nucleic acids in the body's cells. Some foodstuffs are particularly rich in nucleic acids, including liver and kidneys.

Urticaria A skin reaction characterized by weals similar to those caused by nettle rash.

Valerian A herbal preparation used in the treatment of anxiety and emotional tension.

Varix A dilated section of a varicose vein. Varices appear as 'torturous knots' on the vein.

Vasodilation The expansion of the diameter of a blood vessel so that the blood supply is increased.

Vasoconstriction The narrowing of a blood vessel so that the blood supply is reduced.

Vitulograph A machine which measures a patient's lung capacity.

Wernicke's encephalopathy A neurological and psychiatric condition related to a deficiency in vitamin B1 (thiamine) either as a result of malnutrition or alcoholism, or very often both.

Yeast The organisms which cause fermentation of sugars, including those found in grapes and other fruits.

Bibliography

General

Anderson, D., *Drinking to Your Health*, Social Affairs Unit, 1989.

Barr, A., *Wine Snobbery*, Faber and Faber, 1988.

Bender, D. A. and Bender, A. E., *Nutrition, A Reference Handbook*, Oxford University Press, 1997.

Briers, R. and Briers, A., *A Taste of the Good Life*, Pavilion, 1995.

British Medical Association Complete Family Health Encyclopedia, B.C.A. by arrangement with Dorling Kindersley, 1995.

Burton, R., *The Anatomy of Melancholy*, Dell, F. and Jordan-Smith, P. (eds) Tudor Publishing Company, *c*. early to mid-17th century.

Colman, V., *Addicts and Addictions*, Piatkus, 1986.

De Vries, J., *Stomach and Bowel Disorders*, Mainstream Publishing, 1993.

Durkan, A. and Cousins, J., *The Beverage Book*, Hodder and Stoughton, 1995.

Endmann, R. and Jones, M., *Fats, Nutrition and Health*, Thorsons, 1990.

Gelder, M., Gath, D. and Mayou, R., *The Concise Oxford Textbook of Psychiatry*, Oxford University Press, 1994.

Goodwin, D., *Is Alcoholism Hereditary?*, Oxford University Press, 1976.

Institute of Masters of Wine, *Journal of Wine Research*, Carfax Publishing Company, 1996.

Jefford, A. (ed.), *1991 Which? Wine Guide, Which?* Books, 1991.

Jones, A., *Wine Talk*, Piatkus, 1996.

Jones, F., *The Save Your Heart Wine Guide*, Headline Book Publishers, 1995.

Lockhart, R. B., *Scotch Whisky*, Neil Wilson Publishing, 1951.

Maclean, C., *Discovering Scotch Whisky*, NewLifeStyle Publishing Ltd, 1996.

Maury, F., *Your Good Health*, Souvenir Press, 1993.

The Merck Manual (16th edn), Merck Research Laboratories, 1992.

Meyer, M.-L., *Drinking Problems = Family Problems*, Momenta Publishing Ltd, 1982.

Norrie, P., *Medical Roots of a Great Wine Industry*. Australian Wine Foundation.

Preedy, V. R. and Watson, R. R. (eds), *Alcohol and the Gastrointestinal Tract*, CRC Press, 1996.

Protz, R., *The Ale Trail*, Eric Dobby Publishing, 1995.

Rossiter, F. M., *The Practical Guide to Health: A Popular Treatise on Anatomy, Physiology, and Hygiene, with a Scientific Description of Diseases, their Causes and Treatment*, Signs Publishing Company, 1913.

Rowe, C. J. and Mink, W. D., *An Outline of Psychiatry* (10th edn), Brown and Benchmark, 1993.

Bibliography

Sheehy, T. W., 'Alcohol and the Heart: How It Helps, How It Harms'. *Postgraduate Medicine*, Vol. 41, No. 5, pp. 271–7, 1992.

Taylor, J. and Hale, R. (eds), *The Wine Quotation Book*, Robert Hale, 1989.

Unwin, T., *Wine and the Vine*, Routledge, 1991.

Veenstra, J., *Moderate Alcohol Consumption and the Risk of Coronary Heart Disease*, Netherlands Heart Foundation, 1991.

Verschuren, P. M. (ed.), *Health Issues Related to Alcohol Consumption*, ICSI Press, 1993.

Waugh, A., *In Praise of Wine*, Cassell & Company, 1959.

Weatherall, D. J., Ledingham, J. G. G. and Warrell, D. A., *The Oxford Textbook of Medicine* (2nd edn), Oxford University Press, 1987.

Wesley, J., *Primitive Physic. An Easy and Natural Method of Curing Most Diseases*, 1812.

White, S., *Russia Goes Dry*, Cambridge University Press, 1996.

Winton, F. R. and Bayliss, L. E., *Human Physiology*, J. & A. Churchill Ltd, 1949.

Youngson, R., *The Antioxidant Health Plan*, Thorsons, 1994.

Specialist

Ahmed, F. E., 'Toxicological Effects of Ethanol on Human Health'. *Critical Views in Toxicology*, Vol. 25, No. 4, pp. 347–67, 1995.

The Alcohol–Gout Connection. Volume 13, Number 2, 1989.

Altura, B. M. and Altura, B. T., 'Alcohol, Stroke and the Cerebral Circulation'. *Alcohol Health and Research World*, Vol. 14, No. 4, pp. 322–31, 1990.

Anderson, P., Cremona, A., Paton, A., Turner, C. and Wallace, P., 'The Risk of Alcohol' *Addiction*, Vol. 88, No. 11, pp. 1493–508, 1993.

Baker, K. G., Halliday, G. M., Kril, J. J. and Harper, C. G., 'Chronic Alcoholics Without Wernicke-Korsakoff Syndrome or Cirrhosis Do Not Lose Serotonergic Neurons in the Dorsal Raphe Nucleus'. *Alcoholism: Clinical and Experimental Research*, Vol. 20, No. 1, pp. 61–6, 1996.

Beilin, L. J., 'Alcohol and Hypertension in Western Australian Men'. *Australian and New Zealand Journal of Medicine*, Vol. 14, pp. 463–9, 1984.

Bianchi, C., Negri, E., La Vecchia, C. and Franceschi, S., 'Alcohol Consumption and the Risk of Acute Myocardial Infarction in Women'. *Journal of Epidemiology and Community Health*, Vol. 47, No. 4, pp. 308–11, 1993.

Drewer, C., 'Alcohol and the Elderly'. *British Medical Journal*, Vol. 299, 29 July 1989.

Casswell, S., 'Public Discourse on the Benefits of Moderation: Implications for Alcohol Policy Development'. Alcohol and Public Health Research Unit, University of Auckland, New Zealand.

Centre for Rheumatic Diseases, Glasgow Royal Infirmary, 'Alcohol and Response to Treatment of Gout'. *British Medical Journal*, Vol. 296, No. 6637, pp. 1641–2, 1988.

Christian, J. C., Reed, T., Carmelli, D., Page, W. F., Norton, J. A. Jr. and Breitner, J. C. S., 'Self-Reported Alcohol Intake and Cognition in Aging Twins'. *Journal of Studies on Alcohol*, Vol. 56, No. 4, pp. 414–16, 1995.

Day, C. P., 'Alcohol-Risks and Mechanisms of Damage'. Medical Research Council Clinician Scientist Fellow, Newcastle University.

Day, G. L., Blot, W. J., McLaughlin, J. K. and Fraumeni, J. F., Jr. 'Carcinogenic

To Your Good Health!

Risk of Dark vs. Light Liquor'. International Union Against Cancer.

Delin, C. R. and Lee, T. H., 'Drinking and the Brain: Current Evidence'. *Alcohol and Alcoholism*, Vol. 27, No. 2, pp. 117–26, 1992.

Drake, A. I., Butters, N., Shear, P. K., Smith, T. L., Bondi, M., Irwin, M. and Schuckit, M. A., 'Cognitive Recovery with Abstinence and its Relationship to Family History for Alcoholism'. *Journal of Studies on Alcohol*, Vol. 56, No. 1, pp. 104–9, 1995.

Di Sclafani,V., Ezekiel, F., Meyerhoff, D. J., MacKay, S., Dillon, W. P., Weiner, M. W. and Fein, G., 'Brain Atrophy and Cognitive Function in Older, Abstinent Alcoholic Men'. *Alcoholism: Clinical and Experimental Research*, Vol. 19, No. 5, pp. 1121–6, 1995.

Farinati, F., Turatello, F., Fanton, M. C., Della Libera, G., Valiante, F., De Maria, N., Di Mario, F. and Naccarato, R., 'Chronic Atrophic Gastritis: What is the Pathogenetic Role of Alcohol Abuse and Smoking?' *Alcologia*, Vol. 4, No. 1, pp. 23–8, 1992.

Finnigan, F., Hammersley, R. and Millar, K., 'The Effects of Expectancy and Alcohol on Cognitive-Motor Performance'. Behavioural Sciences Group, Faculty of Medicine, University of Glasgow.

Frankland, A. W., personal communications, Guys and St Thomas's Hospital.

Gavaler, J. S. and Van Thiel, D. H., 'The Association between Moderate Alcoholic Beverage Consumption and Serum Estradiol and Testosterone Levels in Normal Postmenopausal Women: Relationship to the Literature'. Departments of Medicine and Surgery, University of Pittsburgh School of Medicine and Department of Epidemiology, University of Pittsburgh.

Goldberg, D. M., Hahn, S. E. and Parkes, J. G., 'Beyond Alcohol: Beverage Consumption and Cardiovascular Mortality'. *Clinica Chimica Acta*, Vol. 237, No. 102, pp. 155–87, 1995.

Govini, S., Trabucchi, M., Cagianoa, R. and Cuomo, V., 'Alcohol and the Brain: Setting the Benefit/Risk Balance'. Institute of Pharmacological Sciences, University of Milano, Department of Experimental Medicine and Biochemical Science, University of Roma Tor Vergata, Institute of Pharmacology, University of Bari.

Guralnik, J. M. and Kaplan, G. A., 'Predictors of Healthy Aging: Prospective Evidence from the Alameda County Study'. *American Journal of Public Health*, Vol. 79, No. 6, pp. 703–8, 1989.

Hanaoka, T., Tsugane, S., Ando, N., Ishida, K., Kakegawa, T., Isono, K., Takiyama, W., Takagi, I., Ide, H., Watanabe, H. and Iizuka, T., 'Alcohol Consumption and Risk of Oesophageal Cancer in Japan: A Case-Control Study in Seven Hospitals'. *Japanese Journal of Clinical Oncology*, Vol. 24, No. 5, pp. 241–6, 1994.

Jepson, R. G., Fowkes, F. G. R., Donnan, P. T. and Housley, E., 'Alcohol Intake as a Risk Factor for Peripheral Arterial Disease in the General Population in the Edinburgh Artery Study'. *European Journal of Epidemiology*, Vol. 11, No. 1, pp. 9–14, 1995.

Knupfer, G., 'Abstaining for Foetal Health: The Fiction that Even Light Drinking is Dangerous'. Alcohol Research Group, Berkeley, CA.

Lip, G. Y. H. and Beevers, G., 'Alcohol, Hypertension, Coronary Disease and

Stroke'. Department of Medicine, University of Birmingham.

Maynard, A. and Godfrey, C., 'Alcohol Policy – Evaluating the Options'. Centre for Health Economics, University of York.

Mufti, S. J., Eskelson, C. D., Odeleye, O. E. and Nachiappan, V., 'Alcohol Associated Generation of Oxygen Free Radicals and Tumour Promotion'. *Alcohol and Alcoholism*, Vol. 28, No. 6, pp. 621–38, 1993.

Noble, E. P., 'The Gene that Rewards Alcoholism'. *Scientific American*.

Palomaki, H. and Käste, M., 'Regular Light-to-Moderate Intake of Alcohol and the Risk of Ischemic Stroke. Is There a Beneficial Effect?' *Stroke*, Vol. 24, No. 12, pp. 1828–32, 1993.

Paunio, M., Höök-Nikanne, J., Kosunen, T. U., Vainio, U., Salaspuro, M., Mäkinen, J. and Heinonen, O. P., 'Association of Alcohol Consumption and Helicobacter Pylori Infection In Young Adulthood and Early Middle Age Among Patients with Gastric Complaints'. *European Journal of Epidemiology*, Vol. 10, No. 2, pp. 205–9, 1994.

Plant, M. A., Bagnall, G. and Foster, J., 'Teenage Heavy Drinkers: Alcohol-Related Knowledge, Beliefs, Experiences, Motivation and the Social Context of Drinking'. From Alcohol Research Group, Department of Psychiatry, University of Edinburgh, Morningside Park, Edinburgh.

Plant, M. A., Bagnall, G., Foster, J. and Sales, J., 'Young People and Drinking: Results of an English National Survey'. *Alcohol and Alcoholism*, Vol. 25, No. 6, pp. 685–90, 1990.

Preedy, V. R., Siddiq, T., Why, H. and Richardson, P. J. 'The Deleterious Effects of Alcohol on the Heart: Involvement of Protein Turnover'. *Alcohol and Alcoholism*, Vol. 29, No. 2, pp. 141–7, 1994.

Rimm, E. B., Chan, J., Stampfer, M. J., Colditz, G. A. and Willett, W. C., 'Prospective Study of Cigarette Smoking, Alcohol Use, and the Risk of Diabetes in Men'. From the Harvard School of Public Health, Boston, USA.

Rimm, E. B., Klatsky, A., Grobbee, D. and Stampfer, M. J., 'Review of Moderate Alcohol Consumption and Reduced Risk of Coronary Heart Disease: Is the Effect due to Beer, Wine or Spirits?' *British Medical Journal*, Vol. 312, No. 7033, pp. 731–6, 1996.

Rubin, E. and Urbano-Marquez, A., 'Alcoholic Cardiomyopathy'. Department of Pathology and Cell Biology, Jefferson Medical College, Philadelphia, and the Alcohol Research and Cardiac Units, Department of Medicine, Hospital Clinic, University of Barcelona.

Simon, J. A. 'Treating Hypertension: The Evidence from Clinical Trials'. *British Medical Journal*, Vol. 313, No. 7055, p. 437, 1996.

Smith, S. J., Deacon, J. M., Chilvers, C. E. D. and Members of the UK National Case-Control Study Group, 'Alcohol, Smoking, Passive Smoking and Caffeine in Relation to Breast Cancer Risk in Young Women'. *British Journal of Cancer*, Vol. 70, No. 1, pp. 112–19, 1994.

Srivastava, L. M., Vasisht, S., Agarwal, D. P. and Goedde, H. W., 'Relation Between Alcohol Intake, Lipoproteins and Coronary Heart Disease: The Interest Continues'. Department of Biochemistry, AllIndia Institute of Medical Sciences, New Delhi, and Institute of Human Genetics, University of Hamburg.

To Your Good Health!

Stewart, S., Finn, P. R. and Pihl, R. O., 'The Effects of Alcohol On The Cardiovascular Stress Response in Men at High Risk for Alcoholism: A Dose Response Study'. Department of Psychology, McGill University, Montreal.

Tarter, R. E., Jacob, T. and Bremer, D. L. 'The Impairment of Cognitive Skills in Sons of Alcoholics'. *The Brown University Digest of Addiction Theory and Application*, Vol. 9, No. 4, pp. 2–3, 1990.

Volpe, A. and Kastenbaum, R., 'Beer and TLC'. *American Journal of Nursing*, Vol. 67, No. 1, pp. 100–103, 1967.

Weisse, M. E., Eberly, B. and Person, D. A., 'Wine as a Digestive Aid: Comparative Antimicrobial Effects of Bismuth Salicylate and Red and White Wine'. *British Medical Journal*, Vol. 311, No. 7021, pp. 1657–60, 1995.

World, M. J., Ryle, P. R. and Thomson, A. D., 'Alcoholic Malnutrition and the Small Intestine'. *Alcohol and Alcoholism*, Vol. 20, No. 2, pp. 89–124, 1985.

Index

abdominal pain, 84, 108, 157
absolute alcohol *see* ethyl alcohol
abstinence: and alcoholism, 19, 144–5, 152; and blood pressure, 64; and cancer, 139; and delirium tremens, 123, 124; and development of gallstones, 86; in Europe, 166–7; and liver disease, 106–7; in old age, 130; very few medical indications for, 18
accident figures, 10
acetaldehyde, 92, 97, 104
acetate, 92
'acid-brash', 78
acne rosacea, 102
acute alcohol poisoning, 93–4, 119, 182
ADH *see* alcohol dehydrogenase
adrenaline, 176, 177
age, and handling alcohol, 11
aggression, 155–6
alcohol dehydrogenase (ADH), 80–81, 92, 104, 161
alcohol tolerance, variations in, 5
alcoholic cardiomyopathy, 51, 54–5; and abstinence, 19; signs and symptoms, 55
alcoholic dementia, 122
alcoholic flushing, 92, 178–9
alcoholism: and abstinence, 19, 144–5, 152; aetiology, 150; Alpha, 146–7; Beta, 147; child, 181; defined, 146; early-onset, 151–2; as easier to prevent than cure, 150; Epsilon, 149; four basic pretexts, 154–5; Gamma, 147–8, 149; and infertility, 70; inheritance of,

151–2; late-onset, 152; and malnourishment, 105, 135, 157; misuse of the term, 145–6; and pancreatitis, 83; and polyneuropathy, 126; in Russia, 108
'alcopops', 186
The Ale Trail (Protz), 25
Alka Seltzer, 99
allergic rhinitis, 173
allergy, 171–80
allopurinol, 116, 117
Alpha alcoholics, 146–7
Alzheimer's disease, 128
American Journal of Medicine, 128
American Journal Of Public Health, 73
American Medical Association, 146
American National Institute of Alcoholism and Alcohol Abuse, 130
amphorae, 23
anaemia, 161, 162, 189
anaphylactic shock, 176
anaphylaxis, 176, 177
The Anatomy of Melancholy (Burton), 86–7
anger, release of, 18
angina, 34, 57, 58
animal experiments, 51
Antabuse, 74
anti-coagulants, 57, 64
anti-depressants, 132
anti-diarrhoeal preparations, 99
anti-inflammatory drugs, 116, 171
anti-psychotic drugs, 125, 129
antihistamines, 171, 172, 178
antioxidants, 31, 33, 34, 38; flavonoids, 35, 60; Mediterranean